Introduction to Healthcare Delivery Organizations

Functions and Management

Fourth Edition

Robert M. Sloane

Beverly LeBov Sloane

Richard K. Harder

Introduction to Healthcare Delivery Organizations

Functions and Management

Fourth Edition

Health Administration Press
Chicago, Illinois

03   02   01   00   99   5   4   3   2   1

Library of Congress Cataloging-in-Publication Data

Sloane, Robert M.
  Introduction to healthcare delivery : organization, functions, and management / Robert M. Sloane, Beverly LeBov Sloane, Richard K. Harder. — 4th ed.
       p.   cm.
  Includes bibliographical references and index.
  ISBN 1-56793-106-5 (alk. paper)
  1. Health facilities. 2. Health facilities—Administration. I. Sloane, Beverly LeBov. II. Harder, Richard K. III. Title
RA963.S533   1999
362.1'068—dc21   97-14524
                                                                  CIP

Previously published as *Guide to Health Care Facilities: Personnel and Management, Third Edition*

The paper used in this publication meets the minimum requirements of American National Standard for Information Sciences—Permanence of Paper for Printed Library Materials, ANSI Z39.48-1984.™

Health Administration Press
A division of the Foundation
  of the American College of
  Healthcare Executives
One North Franklin Street, Suite 1700
Chicago, IL 60606-3491
312/424-2800

In Loving Memory
of
Myrna Leslie Lebov

Contents

Preface

The lack of formal, concise information about the functions and interrelationships of a healthcare organization's personnel—the healthcare team—and its many departments has resulted in a serious gap in the education of members of that team. Many team members who are or will be in supervisory positions also find that information on effective management is lacking. This book is intended to fill such gaps; to offer some basic information on the growth and development of the healthcare organization, and on automation and computer applications; and to provide a look into the future of healthcare organizations.

This book is written for students in the many medical and allied health schools, as well as for persons at all levels and in all professions and vocations who are now employed by, or associated with, healthcare organizations. The governing board member of a healthcare organization may find this book especially useful in easing orientation to the facility. The architect, attorney, accountant, consultant, and sales representative associated with healthcare organizations should also benefit from much of this book in relating to other members of the healthcare team. Finally, we hope that high-school students will become intrigued by this material and pursue the possibility of a rewarding health career.

We are indebted to a number of individuals who have helped greatly in the research and compilation of material. Without their invaluable assistance, this fourth edition would not be a reality. We wish to express our sincere appreciation to the following individuals for their assistance.

David Lynn helped greatly in the research and updating of Part IV, Automation in the Healthcare Organization. David received his master's degree in healthcare and hospital administration from Duke University. He has more than 20 years of experience in healthcare administration and consulting and has been engaged in several international consulting projects on healthcare information. At this writing, he is a fifth-semester doctoral student in public administration at the University of La Verne in La Verne, California.

We are most grateful to Stuart A. Wesbury, Ph.D., president of the
American College of Healthcare Executives from 1979 until 1991 and currently Research Professor at the School of Health Administration of Arizona State University. Dr. Wesbury wrote the final chapter of this book.

The late Duane A. Carlberg, former president/chief executive officer
and colleague, Inter-Community Medical Center, Covina, California, is
remembered. His shared vision, wisdom, and practical healthcare management insights have contributed greatly to Richard Harder's writing of this
book's management chapters.

We thank Adalyn Watts and Sherri L. Smith, who provided off-campus
library services at the University of La Verne Wilson Library (La Verne,
California) for their time and invaluable assistance with the literature searches
for this edition. Our thanks also go to the audiovisual department of Good
Samaritan Hospital (Los Angeles, California) for most of the photographs in
this book.

Part I

Recent History and Development of the Healthcare Organization

Modern Healthcare Organizations— Past and Present

From the first ancient Greek hospital to today's modern healthcare organization, change—progression, regression, innovation—has been a constant. While more change—and progress—has occurred in the last 100 years than in the preceding 2,000, the past few decades have seen dramatic new developments, both in the way diseases are identified and treated and in the way healthcare is delivered to patients. This chapter is an overview of those major catalysts—discovery of anesthesia, sterilization, x-rays, etc.—that not only modernized medicine but initiated the need for more efficient healthcare delivery. The subsequent incarnations of healthcare delivery, such as health maintenance organizations (HMOs) and preferred provider organizations (PPOs), are briefly discussed as well as the classifications—investor-owned or not for profit, specialty or general, government or nongovernment, and long term or short term—under which today's healthcare organizations are governed.

MODERN HEALTHCARE ORGANIZATIONS—THE PAST

The Roots of Modern Healthcare Delivery and Technology

Although the hospital has taken many forms in the past, the evolution of the *modern* healthcare organization can be traced directly to World Wars I and II. Improvised hospitals such as tents, ambulances, ships, trains, and airplanes provided effective medical care to combat soldiers. Progress was made in moving many convalescent patients great distances, and procedures to control contagious diseases were refined to such a degree that the civilian population promptly followed the military example.

Another important development that greatly affected how healthcare is delivered was the Hill–Burton Act. Enacted in 1946 as the Hospital Survey and Construction Act, this legislation authorized grants for states to construct new hospitals and, later, to modernize old ones. This resulted in a boom of hospital construction (and federal reimbursement), the effects of which are still being felt today.

In addition, passage in 1965 of the Social Security Amendments, which brought Medicare and Medicaid into existence, greatly changed how healthcare organizations were reimbursed. Recent attempts to modify—or curtail—such reimbursement still continue to affect healthcare organizations.

Although these changes have had drastic affects on how healthcare is provided, technological innovations—the roots of which stretch back to the nineteenth century—have had a far more tangible impact on patients.

Major Technological Developments

Rapid progress in medicine during the middle and latter parts of the nineteenth century and during the twentieth century revolutionized the healthcare organization. Perhaps the most important development, however, was the discovery and use of anesthesia. Although many operations were performed in the early nineteenth century, patients suffered greatly from the pain of surgery, and surgeons had to work as quickly as possible. The earliest record of using anesthesia was in 1842 when Dr. Crawford Long used ether. In 1844, nitrous oxide was administered by Forest Wells, a dentist in Hartford, Connecticut. Another dentist, William Morton, administered ether before an operation conducted at Massachusetts General Hospital in 1846. In 1847, Sir James Simpson found chloroform to be successful in deadening labor pains. All of these individuals deserve credit for the discovery that enabled surgery as a skilled specialty to progress at a rapid rate and new operative procedures to be devised.

In 1864, Louis Pasteur's research proved both that bacteria are living microorganisms that increase not spontaneously but through reproduction and that they can be destroyed by heat and chemicals. In doing so, he laid the foundation for the modern study of bacteriology. Pasteur studied a condition in wine that was making it sour and unpalatable, and he discovered that the wine was being spoiled by parasitic growths that could be destroyed by heating. He soon extended this process into other fluids, which still bears his name: pasteurization. After 20 years of research into the biology of microorganisms, Pasteur began studying human diseases. In 1885, he developed a vaccine to prevent rabies.

In the 1860s, Joseph Lister discovered a relationship between Pasteur's discovery—that bacteria are present everywhere in the air—and wound infection. Although the need for cleanliness had been known since early times, wound infections were common and expected. Lister began to apply this discovery by protecting open fractures against bacteria with carbolic acid (a disinfectant). He first published his results in 1867, and soon carbolic acid was used in surgery and its application was called the "antiseptic principle." Antisepsis reduced the mortality rate in Lister's hospital after 1865 from 45 percent to 12 percent, and it prepared the way for aseptic surgery.

Continuing this trend, in the 1880s and 1890s, physical sterilization through the use of steam was introduced and developed. This technological advance had a major impact not only in surgery but throughout the hospital, where certain equipment and supplies had to be free of contamination.

The sterile operative technique was further advanced through the introduction of rubber gloves in surgery in 1898 by William S. Halsted. Other advances included special gowns, which came at the turn of the century, and masks, which appeared in the late 1920s. Antibiotics and other drugs helped cut mortality caused by postoperative infection to less than 3 percent in most hospitals.

In 1895, well-known physicist Wilhelm Roentgen discovered that when an electric current was passed through a certain type of tube (which was covered with black paper and some crystals), it began to fluoresce. Using a screen of the same material, Roentgen placed his hand in front of it and saw the shadows of bones on the screen. By replacing the screen with a photographic plate, he obtained a permanent picture. The discovery of the x-ray was published in 1895, and the technology was widely accepted.

The quality of medical education varied widely at the beginning of this century. Because schools were unaccredited, no specific standards existed to follow. The American Medical Association (AMA) (see appendix) was reorganized in 1901, and one of its primary purposes was to elevate the standards of medical education. As a result, in 1904, later the AMA established the Council on Medical Education to inspect and classify medical schools. The investigation and its disclosures led to the Carnegie Foundation for the Advancement of Teaching, which undertook a study of all medical schools in the United States and Canada. The foundation asked Abraham Flexner to make the study; the report, which was published in 1910, led to the closing of a number of schools and to substantial changes in others. Many medical schools were forced to affiliate with hospitals to provide clinical training, but most of them merged with universities and continued their mission under university control.

The twentieth century has produced many advances in laboratory testing. Equipment that allows the rapid laboratory processing of diagnostic and prognostic examinations has been developed, and the number of such examinations has increased dramatically. The simple laboratory set-up found at the beginning of the twentieth century has evolved into a complex department subdivided into many sections. The introduction of studies of prothrombin time in 1940, electrolytes in 1941–1946, blood gas in 1957, creatine phosphokinase in 1961, radioimmunoassay for measuring blood thyroid in 1965, a test for serum hepatitis in 1970, and the first commercially available cancer screening test (carcinoembryonic antigen) in 1974 are just a few of the hundreds of examples of laboratory tests that have been developed during the last several decades. Research continues to add others to the vast array of diagnostic laboratory tests available to today's physician.

In 1916, laboratory workers found that anticoagulating substances allowed blood to be kept refrigerated for two weeks in glass bottles. At least two decades passed, however, before blood banking was found in many large hospitals in this country. In 1942, the blood bank produced only whole blood and plasma, but, since then, it has become possible for patients to receive whole blood, packed red cells without plasma, platelets, plasma, protein from the plasma, or even specific parts of the protein without the others.

A now-standard diagnostic tool that represents recent advances is the electron microscope. Discoveries of the atomic age first entered the field of medicine in 1946. Today, hundreds of radioactive isotopes are being used as weapons against disease. Radiation therapy, which began with the cobalt bomb in 1952, now comes equipped with powerful machines, such as linear accelerators, that produce as many as 35 million electron volts. A major technological advance in radiation therapy, developed in the 1980s, is that of particle beam therapy, which uses neutrons, protons, and subatomic particles to destroy cancer cells without damaging surrounding tissues. Another recent radiation therapy enhancement is hyperthermia—heating tumors by using ultrasound or magnetic fields.

Diagnostic radiology has also advanced markedly, yielding such new techniques as mammography, ultrasound scintigrams, and scanners since the mid-1970s. An enormous advance first used in 1971 in England is an imaging modality called computed tomography (CT). The first CT scanners were head scanners, which led to the introduction of the whole-body scanner in 1974. These latter scanners obtained cross-sectional x-rays of the entire human body. In 1975, about 300 whole-body and head scanners were in place, while today thousands are being used. In the 1980s, another powerful diagnostic tool was added, magnetic resonance imaging (MRI), that provides a noninvasive imaging technique that uses magnetic and radio frequency fields to record images of body tissues and thus to monitor body chemistry—and it does so without using ionizing radiation.

Chemotherapeutic advances have also been remarkable in recent decades. Many drugs have been perfected and released to combat a number of major illnesses, while many others are in the developmental and testing stages. A cancer-fighting drug, Interferon, which when naturally produced costs upwards of $30,000 per patient, could, when cloned, cost as little as $300 per patient. The 1990s have produced exciting new pharmaceutical products that have had and will have an enormous bearing on our well-being.

Surgical advances have been equally remarkable. Bypass surgery was developed in the 1970s, as were joint replacements. Organs are now successfully transplanted in virtually all major medical centers, and artificial organs are being used on an experimental basis. New surgical techniques have included the use of lasers in ophthalmology, gynecology, and other surgical specialties. Microsurgery has become a common tool for vascular and nerve reconstruction. The use of robotics in surgery has been refined and approved in 1998 with new amazing advances planned for the coming years (see Figure 1.1).

The last several decades have witnessed the greatest number of medical advances in the history of medicine. Although such developments have been remarkable, the decades ahead will certainly see even more profound contributions.

MODERN HEALTHCARE ORGANIZATIONS—THE PRESENT
Current Trends in Healthcare Delivery

The way that patients receive healthcare today reflects the dramatic developments in medical technology. The hospital of the past has undergone extensive changes that allow healthcare to be delivered more effectively—and less expensively. Ambulatory care centers have grown steadily over the last decade. Ambulatory care includes those facilities or organizations that provide home health care, outpatient surgery, urgent and emergency care, outpatient rehabilitation and therapy, preventive health and fitness, hospice care, and other diagnostic or therapeutic services on an outpatient basis, as well as the physician's or group practice offices. Led by the increasing pressure for cost containment—and the advent of managed care—and by diagnosis-related group (DRG) reimbursement from Medicare rather than cost reimbursement, the hospital length of stay has decreased dramatically and the number of ambulatory centers has grown sharply.

Other major healthcare delivery developments include the continued growth of HMOs, the formation of PPOs, increased growth of skilled

Figure 1.1   Robotic Surgery

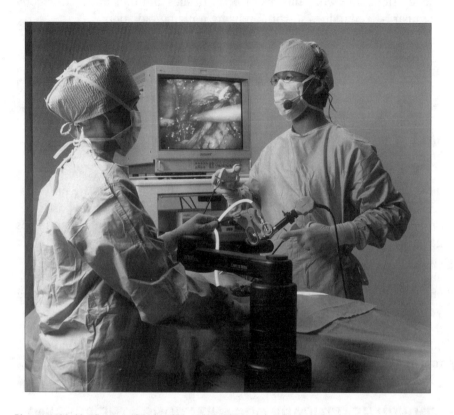

Photo provided by Computer Motion, Inc. (Goleta, CA)

nursing facilities, and extended care beds (subacute) either at the hospital or in a freestanding special facility. The need for additional nursing homes is also evident as acute-care hospitals seek to decrease the length of stay by providing for a more rapid discharge. With safe medical practice in mind, the acute-care institution, and the patient's doctor, desire to keep the hospital stay as short as possible.

Due to various trends and influences, many more types of healthcare organizations have appeared in the last few years. A brief description of several of these follows.

The health maintenance organization

HMOs are health insurance plans that emphasize comprehensive care under a prepaid single insurance premium and use a variety of devices to control cost and quality. Facilities, often integrated with the hospital, clinic, and doctors' offices, are either located in a number of locations or located centrally. Because HMOs are often able to control utilization better than fee-for-service providers, they are lower-cost providers in many communities. The number of HMOs in the United States was approximately 645 in 1997 with more than 81 million enrollees in that year. The largest HMO is the Kaiser Permanente Medical Care Program, with headquarters in Oakland, California, and 8.6 million enrollees in January 1999. Begun in 1933 by Sidney Garfield for California construction workers, Kaiser Permanente now (in 1999) operates in 17 states and the District of Columbia.

Home health care

Home health care is a logical extension of hospital services and has become a widely recognized component of the healthcare delivery system. Home health care services are appropriate for individuals who do not need intensive, full-time care or supervision in an institutional setting but who cannot, without undue hardship, get to needed services on an ambulatory basis.

Preferred provider organizations

PPOs are managed care organizations that offer integrated delivery systems (i.e., networks of providers) that are available through a vast array of health plans and are readily accountable to purchasers for cost, quality, access, and services associated with their networks. They use provider selection standards, utilization management, and quality-assessment techniques to complement negotiated fee reductions in an effective strategy for long-term cost savings. Under a PPO benefit plan, covered individuals retain the freedom of choice of providers but are given financial incentives (i.e., lower out-of-pocket costs) to use the preferred provider network. Preferred provider organizations are marketed directly to employers as well as to insurance companies and third-party administrators, who then market the network to their employer clients (Medicom International 1998).

Walk-in medical clinics

Another type of healthcare delivery organization is the walk-in medical clinic, which can be found in shopping malls and on main thoroughfares and are offered as alternatives to doctors' offices and hospital emergency rooms. They are known primarily as urgent care centers. There are also thousands of freestanding ambulatory surgical centers.

Price competition is the primary reason behind the appearance of walk-in clinics. They are organized and staffed for the hours of profitability only and, in most cases, are not open late in the evening or during the night and early morning hours. The walk-in concept creates a highly favorable pricing structure as an alternative to hospital facilities for many, but certainly not all, procedures.

Hospice care

A change in approach to care for the dying is taking place in a healthcare organization called a hospice, which tries to combine the elements of a small hospital with the warmth and compassion of a patient's home. It is a setting in which the physical, social, spiritual, and psychological needs of dying patients and their families are met. There is an awareness of and compassion for the dying patient's situation, and he or she is given painkillers as needed; because the situation is observed realistically, potential addiction is not an issue.

A team of physicians, nurses, and social workers, along with religious and psychiatric professionals, work with the family of the patient to administer hospice treatment.

Extended care and rehabilitative organizations

Many hospitals have developed extended care facilities—also called skilled nursing facilities (SNFs)—that serve patient needs after the acute phase of illness has passed. The advantage of providing extended care is an economic one: acute care staffing is no longer necessary in an SNF, but adequate staffing is available to meet the needs of patients while they are recuperating and undergoing rehabilitation.

Nursing homes

Thousands of nursing homes across the country provide services for patients who require custodial care but need only minimal care from a physician. Care provided within nursing homes varies according to the home, but normally it consists of some nursing care and of care by social workers who provide assistance to the patients and their families. Among the many services offered is recreational therapy.

Assisted living for seniors

Any study of modern healthcare organizations needs to address the growing phenomenon of continuum of care for senior citizens. The history of senior housing began with the nonprofit sector supported by private and public funding. Now, in addition to the nonprofit and government organizations, for-profit organizations have entered the arena as well, appealing to an upper-scale senior citizen market. Experts in housing, hospitality, and home health care contribute to a range of services that comprise a continuum of care.

One continuum of care campus may have three distinct living facilities. The first level is the independent living facility, which offers apartments that can be owned by or leased to those who can live without assistance.

Increasing with the growing population of older people, the independent living facility is located on a larger campus of continuum of care. The residents are ensured that they will be moved to the next appropriate level of care if and when needed.

The second level is assisted living for people who are still relatively healthy but can no longer drive or attend to some physical activities, such as shopping or preparing meals. The idea of assisted living is helping people live as independently as possible, while recognizing and addressing the needs and limitations that stand in their way. The housing consists of apartments with relatively small kitchenettes suitable for easy use. There is 24-hour supervision by someone always present to help as needed. In some facilities, nursing and psychiatric care is often contracted for.

The third level is the nursing home for people who need complete care. Thousands of nursing homes across the country provide services to patients who require custodial care but need only minimal care from a physician. Care provided within nursing homes varies according to the home, but normally consists of some nursing care and of care by social workers who provide assistance to the patients and their families, recreational therapy, and various other services.

With this continuum of care, the resident never needs to leave his/her community. From independence to non-skilled nursing to skilled nursing, with an emphasis on the interim level of assisted living, the senior citizen's health and housing needs are being recognized.

Industrial medical clinics

Many corporations provide clinics for their employees that not only offer pre-employment examinations and routine annual examinations but are prepared to treat industrial accidents as they occur. Physicians, nurses, x-ray and laboratory technicians, and clerical personnel staff these clinics.

Health department clinics

Health departments have long been involved in preventive medicine, dissemination of health information, and provision of sanitation standards and inspection services. Clinics run by health departments deal with areas such as sexually transmitted diseases, well-baby care, x-ray examination, and family planning.

Integrated delivery systems

Many of the hospitals and other facilities noted above, as well as physicians' offices, have formed integrated delivery systems that provide a "continuum of care," ensuring that patients get the right care at the right time from the right provider. This continuum from primary care provider to specialist and ancillary provider (under one corporate roof or other organizational structure) ensures that patients receive the appropriate care, thus saving money and delivering increased quality of care (Medicom International 1998).

Other facilities

The variety of healthcare organizations is impressive, and more are being developed as need dictates. Mental health centers are offering psychiatric care to millions of citizens, drug control clinics have developed rapidly to meet problems of abuse, and school infirmaries and health centers are meeting the health needs of students. The professionals in these facilities are contributing, in their own way, to the ultimate goal of improved health for all patients everywhere.

MODERN HEALTHCARE ORGANIZATIONS—
THE STATE OF THE INDUSTRY

The Contemporary Hospital

Hospitals have been classified in many different ways. The most commonly accepted classifications, however, are those based on the illnesses or types of patients treated (clinical) or on the type of ownership and control (either government or nongovernment). Clinical hospitals include general hospitals that treat a variety of illnesses and special facilities that treat only one disease or condition or several types of related illnesses. Included among special hospitals are psychiatric, orthopedic, children's and women's hospitals, and those in which catastrophic diseases are treated.

The classification of hospitals based on ownership and control means that they are either supported by the government or not. Under the government category are federal hospitals, such as military hospitals, the Department of Veterans Affairs hospitals, and the United States Public Health Service hospitals. Other types of government hospitals are those run by the state, county, or city. All government hospitals are supported by tax funds, and they may be either general hospitals or specialized organizations.

Nongovernment hospitals vary in ownership and control. Church hospitals are owned by one of the church organizations. Catholic hospitals are usually founded, organized, and managed as part of the mission of a religious order, whereas hospitals of other denominations or religions usually have a separate governing body. Fraternal hospitals are owned by a fraternal order (e.g., Shriners). The largest group of nongovernmental hospitals are called community hospitals because they are owned and maintained by the community, although they are incorporated under a separate charter. The governing board is representative of the community and relates the community's needs and requirements to the hospital. These "community" hospitals are often spoken of as voluntary institutions, in contrast to government hospitals.

Many hospitals are privately owned and operate for profit; these are called proprietary or investor-owned hospitals. Such a facility is owned by a small, closed group or by a corporation with stockholders. Many of these hospitals belong to large corporate chains.

A hospital's size is commonly measured by the number of beds it contains. This bed breakdown is usually in the form of adult beds and pediatric beds, listed separately, although maternity beds and other special categories also may be listed separately. Now that outpatient services are increasing dramatically and inpatient services are decreasing, another classification—based on the number of outpatient visits—is becoming necessary.

Still another means of classifying hospitals is by the average length of a patient's stay. Under this classification, hospitals are divided into short-term and long-term institutions. The average stay of patients in short-term hospitals is 30 days or less, whereas in long-term hospitals it exceeds 30 days. Most of the short-term institutions are general hospitals, whereas the long-term institutions treat patients hospitalized for psychiatric care; for care of respiratory disease; for physical, mental, and substance abuse rehabilitation; and for other special reasons.

Statistical Breakdown of Hospitals

In the 1999 edition of *Hospital Statistics* (Healthcare InfoSource, Inc., a subsidiary of the American Hospital Association), several interesting statistics were reported for 1997, the latest year for which data are complete. There were 6,097 hospitals in the United States, marking a steady decline during the preceding ten years—6,821 hospitals were reported in 1987. Of the hospitals recorded in 1997, 285 were under federal control and 1,260 were operated by state and local governments.

There were 601 nonfederal psychiatric hospitals, 4 nonfederal tuberculosis and other respiratory disease hospitals, 125 nonfederal long-term general and other special hospitals, and 5,082 nonfederal short-term general and other special hospitals (5,659 in 1987). Of the nongovernmental hospitals, 3,000 were nonprofit, short-term general and other, specialized facilities, and 797 were investor-owned institutions.

The 6,097 hospitals operating in 1997 had a total of 1,035,000 beds, admitted 33,624,000 patients, and had an average daily census of 673,000 (number of patients in hospitals at any one time, or 65 percent of capacity).

The average stay for nonfederal short-term general and other special hospitals was 6.1 days (versus 7.2 days in 1987).

Regarding the outpatient population, 520,600,000 hospital outpatient visits were made in the United States in 1997, an increase of approximately 210 million visits, or 67.6 percent, in the preceding decade. In 1997, there were 4,333,000 employees (full-time equivalents) working in all U.S. hospitals. The total operating expense for all of the facilities rose from $179.6 billion in 1987 to $342.3 billion in 1997.

The number of hospitals decreased (down 11 percent) as did the number of beds (down 17.5 percent) between 1987 and 1997. The number of admissions decreased 2.3 percent, the length of stay decreased 15.3 percent, and the number of personnel increased by 15.8 percent during this ten-year period. It is anticipated that this trend will continue as new developments in technology allow for a shorter length of stay and as many more procedures are performed on an outpatient basis.

The decline in hospital admission caused by the growth of specialty clinics that provide effective treatment on an outpatient basis is more than a trend; it is one of the many current manifestations of the evolution of healthcare. In order for this progress to continue, however, healthcare leaders must be equipped to manage through industry laws and regulations that often seem to be in flux.

REFERENCE

Medicom International. 1998. *Managed Care Interface*. Bronxville, NY: Medicom International.

Part II

Healthcare Organization and Operation

2

Healthcare Organization Leadership— Vision, Mission, Strategy, and Implementation

P atient (consumer) demand for access to quality care in healthcare organizations will continue to increase. Healthcare organization administrators are responsible for cooperating with governing board members, physician staff, managers, and supervisors at all levels within their organizations to develop and implement the vision, mission, and strategies for successful delivery of healthcare services. This diverse clinical and nonclinical leadership must also work together in a variety of complex healthcare organizations, including acute care hospitals, medical clinics, SNFs, and convalescent hospitals. They must ensure that there is a need for the health services that are being provided and that the patients have access to care. These healthcare leaders are responsible for ensuring that their organizations succeed financially and that their organizations comply with a host of federal, state, and local rules, standards, and laws that govern the delivery of health services. The qualities and functions of an effective leader in various hospital teams, such as the governing board, the medical staff, and healthcare administrators, are defined in this chapter. In addition, the chapter highlights the importance of an effective mission statement— and provides an actual sample—with which the leader can guide the organization.

ORGANIZATIONAL VISION AND MISSION STATEMENTS

A healthcare organization's vision and mission statement is developed over time and is very important to the organization's management. It reflects the uniqueness of the organization. Once developed, the statement is then introduced to all healthcare organization "stakeholders"—the patients, community members, governing board members, managers, and all employees.

What Is a Vision and Mission Statement?

Visioning is a process by which visions of the future are created. Highly effective healthcare leaders have the ability to foresee the future of their organizations based on keen insight into past, present, and future events that have, are, and will affect their organizations. They have the further ability to analyze data and recommend strategies regarding the direction of their organizations. This results in a process that ensures that decisions made today will have positive results for the organization in the immediate and near future—ideally in three to five years.

A healthcare organization's mission statement is usually an outcome of a strategic planning process. This process usually involves governing board members, senior management, and other key stakeholders such as patients, community members, and employees. The mission statement defines a clear statement of the vision of the organization—namely, its present and future position in the healthcare market. This statement also typically defines in what "business" the organization is—and is not—engaged. Mission statements also outline formal goals set forth for the organization by senior management.

Sample Mission Statement:
San Antonio Community Hospital
(Upland, California)

"We will provide high quality patient care, services, and facilities that respond to consumer, payer, and physician needs. We will manage our resources cost-effectively and efficiently in order to maintain financial strength which will enable us to sustain and promote our position of leadership in delivering healthcare to people in our service area."

[Used with permission from San Antonio Community Hospital]

**Sample Organizational Philosophy Statement:
Anaheim Memorial Hospital
(Anaheim, California)**

The C.E.O. will drive the hospital's vision. Executive management will be the model by which others follow. Vice Presidents will relinquish as much of their control of daily operations as practical to department heads, who will in turn encourage subordinates' participation in decision making. Interaction between departments and levels will influence faster adaptation to external and internal forces.

Employees at all levels will be empowered—and expected—to use their minds and suggest how AMH can be a more productive and proactive environment. Innovation and creativity will be rewarded. A significant part of managerial performance appraisals will be the extent to which new ideas are developed and implemented within their departments.

The organization will strive to eliminate those policies and meetings that inhibit organizational progress and development. Intelligent risk taking will be encouraged, and decisions will be made and problems will be handled without fear of reprisal.

Customers' needs will be consistently assessed, met, and integrated into all service offerings. An attitude of "Fix it" will prevail, making things easier and more efficient for patients, doctors, and staff.

THE GOVERNING BOARD/TRUSTEE LEADERSHIP

Responsibilities

The responsibilities of the governing board include, but are not limited to, developing organizational policy; establishing bylaws in accordance with the health service organization's legal and licensing requirements; selecting qualified facility administrators; ensuring proper organization of clinical staff; monitoring quality of care; and determining the organization's mission, strategic plan, goals, objectives, and policies to achieve its strategic mission and plans. The healthcare governing board member of the future must be able to address effectively a wide range of stakeholder interests within integrated healthcare delivery systems. Additionally, board members must have the ability to understand and value diverse cultures represented by community members, patients, and employees. Essentially, they must be able to maintain that vision of what their organization must become to succeed in managed care environments, they must be able to compete effectively with the external healthcare environment, and they must engender high levels of trust and cooperation within their organization's internal environments.

The governing board or council, board of trustees, or board of directors has responsibility for organization policymaking. Policy, once formulated, is entrusted to the chief executive officer (CEO) of the institution for implementation.

The governing body's elected officers usually consist of a chairman, vice chairman, president (often the facility's administrator), secretary, and treasurer. Membership size of the governing board varies considerably. Individual members of the governing board—commonly called board members or trustee members—serve on one or more standing committees, commonly the executive committee, joint conference committee, finance committee, strategic planning committee, and building committee. Competition and healthcare reform place high demand on board committees.

The executive committee is empowered by the governing board bylaws to act as the board when the board is not in session. This greatly facilitates policymaking because it would be cumbersome on many occasions to try to arrange the board members quickly for a quorum. This committee reviews some agenda items and reports before they are finally presented to the entire governing board. The joint conference committee, formed from members of the governing board, the administrator, and members of the medical staff, can be the communication vehicle between the board, the administration, and physician staff. Ad hoc committees, often formed for a specific purpose, report back to the entire board.

Composition

Depending on the type of healthcare organization, the governing board should reflect the needs and characteristics of the surrounding community. Because the governing board represents the link between the institution and the community, it is important that the membership represent the entire community. Formerly, "prominent citizens" or large contributors constituted the majority of healthcare organizations' boards, but a more diverse membership results in a more objective representation of the communities served. Members of governing boards—or trustees—provide important strategic leadership and direction to large integrated healthcare networks, for-profit hospital chains, a physician–hospital health facility, or a freestanding community hospital or other type of specialized healthcare organization.

Health facility governing board members (trustees) are now being challenged to expand their skills more than ever before. These skills include keen business acumen and insights regarding business strategy, being able to represent diplomatically opposing and often competing interests and points of view strongly held by key healthcare stakeholder groups, not the least of which are the patients, physicians, payors, and other health disciplines within the systems that they govern.

The continued effects of federal and state healthcare reform, reimbursement constraints, and change in the face of intense healthcare compensation requires that today's governing board members understand and assume their proper role, their organization, and the organization's strategic direction; most importantly, they must maintain a strong emphasis and alliance with the patients being served. Most governing boards have at least one medical staff member (commonly the chief of medical staff). Additional members of the board are also medical staff members and provide valuable input to the board's discussions and decisions.

A Look to the Future—The Changing Role of Healthcare Governance

Governing board members with policymaking and fiduciary responsibility for healthcare organizations will continue to face greater accountability regarding managed care, cost containment, and integration of services to maintain fiscal stability and to ensure the delivery of quality patient care. They will be faced with increased ethical issues related to patient rights, an aging population, advances in healthcare technology, and quality of life.

MEDICAL STAFF LEADERSHIP

Roles and Responsibilities

The medical staff is a significant component of the governing leadership and clinical team in healthcare organizations. These clinically skilled professionals consist of physicians who have received extensive training in a variety of medical disciplines such as family practice, orthopedics, general surgery, oncology, internal medicine, and pediatrics, to name a few. Their primary objective is to diagnose the patient's medical condition accurately and thoroughly and to prescribe the highest-quality and most cost-effective treatment plans. Physician membership on the governing board is valuable to the healthcare organization: Physicians provide important clinical insight related to the strategic and operational decisions this policymaking body makes.

The AMA is the preeminent professional association for physicians. The association's principles includes a physician Code of Medical Ethics developed by the English physician and philosopher Sir Thomas Percival in 1803. This code includes the requirements for members to "strive to expose those physicians deficient in character or competence, or who engage in fraud or deception."

Operationally, the medical staff is the aggregate of physicians of all medical specialties with medical privileges in a healthcare organization. The medical staff's primary objective is to provide the highest quality of care to the patient. Physicians typically organize formally within healthcare organizations to ensure the best possible care, to implement and administer peer review, to ensure quality, to initiate and maintain self-government, to provide a means to solve problems of a medical administrative nature, and to develop and maintain medical staff educational standards.

Classifying medical staff members according to clinical assignments constitutes the organization of the medical staff. Typical medical staff classifications include provisional, honorary, consulting, active, courtesy, or medical resident staff assignments. Depending on the size of the healthcare organization, as well as the credentials and clinical privileges of the staff members, a separation into medicine, surgery, obstetrics, pediatrics, and other specialty services may occur.

Officers of the medical staff usually consist of a president or chief of staff, vice president or chief of staff elect, and a secretary. These offices are authorized by vote of the active medical staff. The president of the medical staff presides at all regular meetings of the medical staff and is, *ex officio*, a member of medical staff committees. In the absence of the president, the vice president assumes all responsibilities and authority of medical committees. The secretary ensures that accurate and complete minutes of all medical staff meetings are maintained and that correspondence is appropriately handled. This is usually done by a medical staff coordinator. In the absence of a treasurer, the secretary receives and is accountable for any funds of the medical staff.

Committee Structure

A well-organized medical staff committee structure can effectively oversee the quality of care being provided to the patients. Because of the increased integration of healthcare organizations, resulting in a increased complexity of healthcare providers and health systems, the traditional line of patient care accountability has become challenging.

Despite significant changes and developments in the organization and structure of health organizations, the responsibility for medical staff committees to monitor and improve quality of care remains the same.

Medical staff committee structures are determined largely on the size and composition of the medical staff and the medical programs of the institution. The body may be divided into committees or it may be small enough to function as a whole. An executive committee coordinates the activities and general policies of the various departments. A credentials committee reviews applications for appointment and reappointment to all categories of the staff. A joint conference committee is a medico-administrative liaison group, or a similar body is in place in most institutions.

Other common standing committees are the pharmacy and therapeutics committee, which serves as a liaison between the pharmacy and medical staff; the program committee, responsible for the program of all meetings; and the medical education committee. Committees also may be formed for special assignments and ongoing functions. The list given here is a synopsis of some of the more important committees and their responsibilities; it is not meant to be all-encompassing.

Graduate Medical Education

Medicine is at the top of the list of the learned occupations and has long been considered the premier healthcare profession. To practice medicine requires advanced skill and training in the health sciences at the very highest levels.

The incremental progression of graduate medical education no longer flows from the traditional clinical clerkship, or externship, to the internship to the residency, or fellowship. Since July 1, 1995, internships as such have stopped being offered and have instead been replaced by the first year of graduate medical education, usually in a specialty medical training program—for example, in surgery or pediatrics. This includes the family practice programs, which are three years in length. Graduate medical training involves direct patient care as opposed to classroom education. To help bridge the gap from classroom to bedside, the clinical clerkship, or externship, introduces a medical student who has not completed academic training to clinical prevention, diagnosis, and treatment of illness.

Advanced clinical experience (residency), with rotation through the various disciplines of medicine such as surgery, pediatrics, and obstetrics, then allows the graduate physician to specialize in a chosen field. The fellowship is similar to a residency in its requirements, but the educational emphasis here is on research.

Physicians are licensed in most states after passing an extensive examination following completion of their residency training. In most cases, the license issued by the state is unrestricted in terms of clinical activities that the physician may undertake. The state medical license essentially authorizes the physician to prescribe medications and perform medical and surgical procedures.

Continuing Medical Education

The medical staff also has the responsibility of offering entry for its membership into appropriate continuing medical education courses. Topics of general value, such as cardiopulmonary resuscitation and infectious disease control, need frequent review. Ideally, the quality assurance/utilization review process can underscore information deficiencies on the part of the medical staff, and these can be converted into enlightening continuing medical education courses for physicians.

A Look to the Future

On an increasing scale, physicians will continue as both the primary caregivers and key partners with healthcare organizations as a result of integration strategies, physician incentives, and joint venture arrangements. The magnitude of managed care in the future, with its impact on financial reimbursement to healthcare providers, will result in increased medical group practices. Solo physician practitioners, much like the freestanding healthcare organization, will seek alliances, mergers, acquisitions, and partnerships to continue the medical practice for which they received their training. To stay competitive, healthcare organizations must seek win-win alliances with physician groups with their patient service areas.

HEALTHCARE ADMINISTRATION LEADERSHIP

Healthcare facility administrators are much like orchestra conductors. Their job is to coordinate, with reasonable levels of organizational harmony and teamwork, the collective talents and efforts of the many key stakeholders in their organizations, including governing board members, medical staff, community members, and service groups.

In large, complex healthcare organizations the administrator/CEO supervises and coordinates the activities of numerous highly specialized and multidisciplined departments performing either medical, administrative, or supportive services. The administrator's staff may include assistants to whom are delegated certain responsibilities and authority. These individuals have such titles as vice president, associate administrator (often the chief operating officer), assistant administrator, or administrative assistant, depending on their scope of responsibility.

The CEO's duties range from coordinating professional services to the patient, building a highly effective management team, and providing timely operations reports to the governing board to initiate new and effective programs that meet community healthcare needs. Progressive executives do not limit their activity to their own institutions. They may be active at the local, state, or national level in professional organizations and may contribute individually to the determination of national healthcare policy.

As healthcare organizations become more complex, the leadership challenges of administrative officers will become increasingly more difficult as they strive to achieve the strategic objectives of their organizations. The job of the administrator (also often called president and/or CEO) is to develop an effective healthcare team consisting of a diverse staff of technically and professionally trained personnel. Examples of these healthcare professionals are physicians, nurses, pharmacists, and a number of highly specialized diagnostic and therapeutic professionals. The administrator/CEO directs the details of daily health service operations and assumes a major role in planning, developing, and expanding new medical services within a highly competitive and volatile business.

In today's managed care environments, in which reimbursement for services has been limited significantly, administrators still must coordinate in a cost-effective manner a wide range of specialized departments performing medical, administrative, or supportive services. The administrator's staff may include individuals with such titles as assistant administrator, chief operating officer, or administrative assistant, depending on the organization's size and scope of individual responsibility.

The administrator's duties range from coordinating professional services to the patient, building effective management teams, and reporting operations activity to the governing board to implementing new and effective programs in response to community needs. Like CEOs, progressive healthcare organization administrators do not focus only on their own institution. They may be active at the local, state, or national level in professional healthcare organizations. They may also contribute individually to the determination of national healthcare policy.

Qualifications

The most common education degree for healthcare administrators is the master's degree. Some programs require two or three years of academic work, while others provide up to a year of practical experience as an administrative resident or intern. While the majority of health service administrators possess an advanced degree—for example, master's of science in health administration (MSHA), master's of health administration (MHA), or master's of public health (MPH), a number will have obtained advanced degrees in other disciplines such as a master's of business administration

(MBA), while others may have a doctorate in an appropriate subject or may have a degree in medicine.

Administrators of some hospitals and healthcare organizations do not have an advanced college degree but may possess a bachelor's degree with an appropriate major or area of concentration. Most medium-to-large healthcare organizations, however, prefer to select administrative staff from those who have completed graduate courses in medical care administration.

The basic curriculum in accredited health services management programs covers assessment and understanding of the health status of a population; the organization, finance, and delivery of health services; economics, finance, and quantitative analysis; ethical issues in the practice of health services administration; information management; leadership; and evaluation methods for determining organizational effectiveness.

Healthcare Organization Leadership— A Look to the Future

Access to health services, cost containment, service quality, and the fiscal viability of healthcare organizations will continue to be the agenda for organizational leaders well into the twenty-first century. Operating a healthcare organization within managed care environments will continue to challenge leaders well into the next decade.

Redefining organizational vision and mission—as well as strategic planning and increased merger, acquisition, and health service integration activity—will continue in the years ahead. Addressing this increased business growth, affiliation, and change and paying continuous attention to cost containment will be necessary for healthcare organizations to deliver quality patient care.

3

Nursing/Patient Care Services

The rapidly changing healthcare system continues to demand skilled nursing personnel with a diverse set of skills and competencies, as well as higher education. The issues of available licensed nursing personnel, basic and continuing educational requirements, and role definition have been debated for over 25 years. Irrespective of the issues of licensing, education, and role definition, the fact remains that nursing professionals continue to be most valued healthcare service providers. They spend more time at the patient's bedside than any other healthcare professional. Their clinical expertise and influence on the overall welfare of the patient is becoming increasingly more dynamic and significant in the managed care health services environment.

In almost every healthcare organization, nursing services (commonly called patient care services) is the single largest clinical department in terms of staff, budget, specialized services offered, and clinical expertise of nursing personnel. Nursing continues to be the largest healthcare occupation in the United States, according to the reports of the U.S. Bureau of the Census Current Population Survey. According to their 1994 report, healthcare organizations employed 1.8 million registered nurses (RNs), 370,000 licensed practical nurses (LPNs), and 1.5 million nurse aides/assistants, orderlies, and attendants (collectively referred to as aids in the healthcare workplace). Another study reported the total number of nurses (RNs) with a license as 2,558,874 in March of 1996, with 2,115,815 (82.7 percent) employed in nursing (Moses, 1997).

Nursing is responsible for providing continuous, around-the-clock health maintenance, treatment, and support of the patient. The quantity and quality of nursing care available to patients is influenced by a number of factors: educational preparation and specialization, experience, and skill level, as well as nursing organization and staffing levels. Nursing service involves identifying timely and expert intervention in response to a wide range of problems related to the patient's treatment, comfort, and safety during the course of the medical treatment plan prescribed by the physician. In essence, this is a process that includes patient assessment, care planning, treatments appropriate to the scope of practice, and evaluation. Most importantly, effective nursing professionals are empathetic and understanding of the patient's feelings and emotions while applying their clinical expertise for the patient's well-being.

In response to the public's increasing health consciousness and the demand for access to quality healthcare, the role of today's nurse has expanded to include patient educator and advocate. Nurses today help patients to increase their understanding of health issues generally and personal health problems specifically. Nursing has clearly shifted from a routine task-oriented job to a multiskilled, multitalented healthcare profession, which is the subject of this chapter.

EMERGENCE OF "DIFFERENTIATED PRACTICE"

For the last decade, prominent nursing educators and nursing service executives in several states have expressed the need to establish a more flexible and adaptable model for nursing practice that is more effective and responsive to patients' healthcare needs. This model—referred to as "differentiated practice"—is a restructuring of nursing roles on the basis of education, experience, and competence. The restructuring of the nursing practice, as well as differentiated formal nursing curriculum and education, is believed to be critical to the future of nursing and to the effectiveness and quality of nursing care to patients.

The managed care movement of the last decade has resulted in a shift in nursing employment from the hospital environment toward nonhospital settings. Because of this trend, nursing educators and institutions are evaluating how well traditional nursing educational institutions are responding to and meeting emerging trends in nursing labor market trends. This results in a greater emphasis placed on differentiated nursing practice mentioned previously, which is essentially about maximizing the utilization of the multiskilled and technically trained nursing professionals in response to the changing healthcare industry.

NURSING EDUCATION AND UTILIZATION

Those interested in the nursing profession can select from among several choices of formal nursing education programs. Following completion of a formal degree program offered by an accredited college or university, the nursing graduate is then eligible to take a state licensing examination. Following satisfactory completion of the state examination, the nursing student then becomes certified as a licensed registered nurse and is eligible to practice in the field of nursing.

Hospital-based Nursing Programs

The length of study in hospital nursing education programs is approximately three years. Understandably, many changes have been made in nursing curriculum content over the years in response to the general health condition of those receiving health services, advances in nursing service technology, and the expanded role of the professional nurse.

Relating the patient care environment to the formal academic learning process is a carefully programmed undertaking. In most nursing school programs, considerable opportunity exists for nursing students to experience clinical practice under direct and indirect supervision. The theory of nursing practice and some general education subjects are included in the curriculum. Students' clinical training prepares them to begin nursing after satisfactory completion of the required state certification examination.

Undergraduate Nursing Programs

Two undergraduate degree programs in nursing are offered by many accredited colleges and universities. The first of these programs is the associate degree program, usually offered by junior or community colleges. This is a full two-year program of study that includes nursing theory together with general undergraduate courses in the liberal arts and sciences. Practice in the clinical setting is provided through contractual arrangements with neighboring hospitals and other healthcare organizations. This program prepares nursing students for entry-level positions in which they will provide direct patient care. The emphasis in this degree is placed on preparation for employment in a variety of healthcare settings other than the acute care hospitals, such as hospice care and home health care agencies, SNFs, and medical offices.

The baccalaureate degree in nursing is offered by accredited four-year colleges and universities, and the program ranges from four to five years (including clinical experience) and provides a general undergraduate education with a nursing major. Because much emphasis is placed on leadership roles and clinical specialties, the graduate of a baccalaureate program in nursing is prepared to practice in a variety of settings. The master's degree in nursing is conferred on those students who have successfully completed graduate courses in the functional areas of education administration. They are called clinical nurse specialists and nurse practitioners. Increasingly, both administrative and clinical nursing positions are held by those with master's degrees in nursing. Clinical nurse specialists practice in areas of critical care, maternal–child health, medical–surgical care, pulmonary care, orthopedics, rehabilitation, and numerous other increasingly complex patient care settings. Their expertise continues to be in high demand in today's healthcare organizations.

Doctoral Nursing Programs

Advanced degrees in nursing, which include doctorate of nursing science (Ph.D. in nursing), prepare the graduate for specialty work in healthcare settings as well as for teaching, research, and administrative positions in college or university settings.

Licensed Practical Nursing Education

The licensed practical nurse or vocational nurse is qualified to care for patients under the direction of an RN or a physician in various healthcare organizations. Although the educational requirements and licensing or certification procedures vary from state to state, high school graduation is usually a prerequisite. To obtain a state license, the practical nurse is expected to complete nine to fifteen months of study in a state-approved school of practical nursing. Emphasis is placed on developing technical skills in patient care.

STATE NURSING LICENSE

An understanding of the purpose of the nursing license may be helpful to understand why graduates of various nursing education programs are required to take a state licensing examination. Nursing education programs differ in objectives, philosophies, curriculum content, and general requirements for completion. Licensing examinations are not based primarily on curriculum content or on the amount of knowledge acquired by a student from a particular type of educational program. Rather, these examinations are concerned directly with the fundamental needs of patients. They are designed to ascertain whether the new practitioner of nursing can distinguish between the safe and the unsafe, the effective and the ineffective in nursing practice. To the extent that such measurements can be accomplished through a written test holding a certain degree of validity and reliability, the examinations are appropriate to the many thousands of nursing students who must be tested each year. Possessing a license to practice marks the professionalism of the nurse.

NURSING SERVICE ORGANIZATION

The Joint Commission on Accreditation of Healthcare Organizations (JCAHO) states that nursing services, including nursing care, are to be provided on a continuous basis, 24 hours a day, 7 days a week, to those patients requiring such care and service. Nursing monitors each patient's status and coordinates the provision of nursing care while assisting other professionals in implementing patient care plans. To accomplish this goal, the hospital provides a sufficient number of qualified nursing staff members to assess the patient's nursing care needs, plan and provide nursing care interventions, prevent complications and promote improvement in the patient's comfort and wellness, and alert other care professionals to the patient's condition as appropriate (JCAHO 1997).

The organized nursing service is usually administered by a registered nurse qualified by advanced education and management experience. Although the title may vary with the role that the administrative head of nursing plays in the total organizational structure, the most often-used title of the key nurse executive is director or vice president of nursing.

This nursing executive's credentials for appointment should include educational preparation, experience as a clinical practitioner and supervisor, and demonstrated ability appropriate to the number and types of health services offered by the healthcare organization. The nursing executive is usually directly responsible to the administrator of the healthcare organization. Authority to administer nursing services must necessarily be delegated to other administrative nursing personnel when one nursing director cannot know and supervise all employees in the department. Thus, a variety of nursing organization patterns exist in today's highly diverse healthcare organizations.

In any nursing organizational structure, several types of relationships can be identified. *Line relationships* identify the positions of superiors and subordinates, indicating levels of authority and responsibility, such as the "higher" relative position of the surgical director with authority to direct the work of several nursing personnel of a surgical unit. *Lateral relationships* define the connection among various positions in which a hierarchy of authority is not involved. For example, the nurse manager of a surgical intensive care unit maintains a lateral relationship with a doctor, a pulmonary physiologist, a dietitian, and others at similar levels.

A third kind of nursing organizational relationship is the *functional relationship,* which occurs when duties are divided according to function. In such arrangements, individuals exercise authority in one particular area by virtue of their special knowledge and expertise. The relationship of the nursing executive with the healthcare organization's fiscal officer or human resource director is an example of the functional relationship. Some administrative personnel use the term *staff* instead of *functional* when discussing organizational relationships, which is certainly an acceptable practice. *Functional* is used here to allow for the inclusion of a fourth nursing relationship—staff relationships—which arise when individuals act on behalf of a superior. For example, in the absence of the nursing executive, the associate director may act in his or her stead, transmitting and interpreting existing policies and procedures and seeing that nursing service is being implemented.

Staffing the Nursing Function
Administrative staff

The preamble to the Code for Nurses, developed by the American Nurses Association (ANA), states that clients are the primary decision makers in matters concerning their own health, treatment, and well-being, and that "the goal of nursing actions is to support the client's responsibility and self-determination to the greatest extent possible" (ANA).

To provide the best possible nursing care for patients and to meet this stated goal of nursing actions, there must be an organized group of administrative nurses responsible for defining the philosophy, goals, and objectives of the department. The organization of the nursing administrative staff, the number and kinds of positions included, and the qualifications of the personnel depend on the size and variety of services offered by the organization.

Joint Commission standards require that the nursing service of an organization be under the direction of a legally and professionally qualified RN and that enough licensed RNs be on duty at all times to give nursing care to patients. The Joint Commission further requires that the nurses use their judgment and specialized skills in planning, assigning, supervising, and evaluating the nursing care of patients. Almost every nursing service has an administrative head who is responsible for organizing the nursing service.

In a large organization, this nurse executive may employ other management-level nurses who function in a supportive line relationship. Such positions would include, for example, assistant or associate directors of nursing, nursing mangers responsible for more than one nursing service, and patient care coordinators (heads of various specialized nursing services such as surgery/recovery, psychiatric services, urgent care, medical/surgical services, intensive care, and home health care services.

Associate or assistant directors of nursing assist in planning with other departments within a healthcare organization and are involved in the coordination of activities and services that contribute to the physical environment and to patient care.

A nursing manager is usually a professional RN who is responsible for nursing care, in a healthcare organization, that involves one or more patient units, each of which has a charge nurse—also commonly referred to as patient care coordinators. Nurse managers generally participate in developing and implementing the philosophy and objectives of nursing service with the nursing executives. They are usually involved in the development and control of capital and operating budgets, the selection of supplies and equipment, and the arrangement and design of physical facilities within their assigned area of work. A nursing manager is usually responsible for planning the kind and amount of patient care that will be given, that is, staffing, analyzing, evaluating, and revising nursing services as needed. Nursing managers are often involved in evaluating nursing employee performance, and they usually take an active part in staff development and in-service educational programs. They coordinate the services of all nursing personnel assigned to the unit under their direction, are usually involved in the evaluation of nursing job performance, and spend much time teaching the unit's nursing staff.

A patient care coordinator (charge nurse) is a registered professional nurse who is usually responsible for the direct and indirect nursing care of patients within an organized unit of a clinical area such as surgery, medicine, or pediatrics, or a specialized unit such as the nursery, the coronary care unit, or emergency room. Patient care coordinators also participate in establishing standards of patient care as well as unit policies and objectives. They accept responsibility for carrying out physicians' orders and for the accurate reporting and recording of patient symptoms, reactions, and progress.

Other nursing staff

A team leader is usually a registered professional nurse who works under the supervision of a patient care coordinator. Other members of the nursing team may include RNs, practical nurses, nurse's aides, orderlies, attendants, messengers, and volunteers. The nursing team is responsible for working with an assigned group of patients and their families in providing, planning for, and evaluating the quality and quantity of direct nursing care. The team leader has varying responsibilities that include direct participation in providing care to selected patients. He or she supervises other nursing team personnel; assists in planning for the teaching and evaluation of the patient, the family, and nursing personnel; and cooperates in the teaching and evaluation functions.

The nursing case manager is responsible for assigning critical pathways for assigned patients. This nursing professional has become increasingly important with the growth of managed care contracts (e.g., flat payment by diagnosis or per day).

The clinical specialist demonstrates a high degree of professional competence in a specialized field of nursing. The qualifications for a clinical specialist usually include a master's degree with a major in nursing and considerable experience in the clinical care of patients. He or she plans, provides for, and controls the nursing care of specific groups of patients who comprise a caseload. To fulfill this responsibility, the clinical specialist must systematically assess the patient, establish a nursing diagnosis, and consider the findings and therapeutic plans of the physician and of others on the health team, as well as define the short-term and long-range goals of nursing care. The clinical specialist functions as a consultant to members of nursing teams and to other health workers. As such, this nursing specialist is expected to be informed about scientific progress in his or her particular specialized field and in the other health professions. The clinical specialist is also expected to find appropriate means for incorporating these new findings into his or her practice. The discharge planning nurse has a very important role in nursing service. This position is usually occupied by a registered nurse with an educational background and experience in community health nursing.

The discharge planning nurse assists the nursing staff in identifying nursing needs that will continue after a patient's discharge from the healthcare organization. He or she also plans and conducts follow-up surveillance after the patient is discharged. The discharge planning nurse facilitates the coordination of care, through referral systems, to appropriate community agencies and institutions, and cooperates with other hospital-based health professionals.

Unit nurse manager

The critical human resources situation facing healthcare organizations has brought about a detailed analysis of possible alternative approaches to the staffing and use of nursing personnel. The unit manager classification represents a new approach to the problem of allocating skilled nursing personnel. The professional nurse has been educated and trained for skilled nursing duties, but the increasingly complex activities of the individual patient division have removed many of these skilled personnel from care of the patient. The RN moving up the ladder of the nursing organization is burdened with performing and delegating increasingly more complicated and time-consuming management and clerical tasks. The unit manager steps in to provide order and administrative direction for the patient unit.

The key to successful unit management is the ability of the unit manager to plan and coordinate unit activities effectively. His or her daily interactions will reach almost every department in the healthcare organization, from direct patient care in radiology or physical therapy to ancillary services, such as laundry and the business office. The unit manager thus becomes the focal point of all non-nursing responsibilities for the patient unit, and the ability of this expert to coordinate these tasks will permit professional nursing personnel to practice patient care more effectively.

Unit secretary

Clerical personnel are increasingly providing valuable assistance to nursing service. If carefully selected and properly trained, the unit secretary can greatly relieve those who are trained to give patient care, enabling them to do their work. Job descriptions of unit secretaries vary greatly but can easily include such responsibilities as controlling all communications to and from a busy nursing station, coordinating patient services, keeping records, and maintaining both the environment and the inventory of supplies. Unit secretaries can be trained to use intensive care and patient intercommunications systems properly. They can provide telephone service, answer incoming calls, take messages, give information within their specified scope of responsibility, request services, and assist with sending and receiving messages. They can receive, sign for, and deliver mail and flowers to patients. They can act as receptionists for patients' relatives or other visitors, for clergy, and for other healthcare personnel. They can post schedules and notices, maintain bulletin boards, and provide continuity for unit desk operations by holding interval reports with nursing clerks coming on duty. They can prepare daily diet changes and nourishment lists and can see that all patient menus are submitted to food and nutritional services. They can notify specialized treatment areas and departments—respiratory therapy, laboratory, radiology, and so on—of specific orders for services.

Specially trained unit secretaries can transcribe doctors' orders for treatment, medication, and laboratory services. They can prepare charts for admission, discharge, and transfer of patients, as well as requisitions for daily laboratory services and other diagnostic tests. Computer-based record-keeping tasks can include patient admission, discharge, and transfer statistics. Additional tasks for unit secretaries may include checking presurgical charts for necessary reports and consents, and following through on missing reports. Orientation can also include learning to chart and graph records of a patient's temperature, pulse rate, respiration, and blood pressure readings reported by nursing personnel. Unit secretaries may be authorized to post laboratory and other diagnostic tests on patients' charts and can play a valuable role in preparing and collecting charge cards (for supplies and other services).

Nursing in Outpatient Services

An outpatient department may be a special area of a healthcare organization, or outpatient care may be the *entire* function of a healthcare organization. Here, a group of professional health personnel coordinate their knowledge, abilities, and skills to provide diagnostic, therapeutic, rehabilitative, and preventive health services to the ambulatory individual who is ill or is seeking help. In an outpatient department, a clinic is a subdivision in which a single disease, or a closely allied group of diseases, is diagnosed and treated. For example, an outpatient department may have clinics specializing in cardiac care, dental care, dermatology, gynecology, neurology, and psychiatric treatment. In highly specialized outpatient departments, a number of medical clinics may be organized to deal with specific medical problems such as diabetes, arthritis, high/low blood pressure, heart disease, and allergies. Regardless of the kind of outpatient department or clinic, daily nursing services are essential. Nursing personnel also are usually responsible for the physical environment (e.g., keeping adequate supplies available in individual examining rooms so that the daily work scheduled there can proceed). They should give particular attention to the physical environment to ensure the comfort and safety of patients waiting and moving through the sometimes intricate systems associated with outpatient departments.

General Nursing Staffing

Enough RNs should be on hand both to direct licensed practical nurses and nurse's aides in carrying out routine tasks and to correlate the competencies of these employees, their levels of experience, and their backgrounds so that the tasks are assigned accordingly. Nurses take particular care in carrying out physicians' directions because medical orders for diagnostic tests and the individual needs of patients scheduled for specific clinics are often complex. Nurses receive and orient patients to clinic routines, and they play a vital role in interpreting physicians' instructions, the appointment systems that prevail, and the movement throughout the healthcare organization for patients undergoing various tests and diagnostic work ups. Nursing personnel assist with examinations of patients, maintenance of records, and scheduling of appointments. They are also responsible for patient and family education, which consists of many aspects that include teaching reasons for and ways to prepare for diagnostic tests and examinations, and providing instruction on how to cope with disease. The present managed care system, as well as restrictions on reimbursement for healthcare services, places significant pressure on healthcare organizations—specifically on nursing services—to adequately staff to provide the volume and quality of patient care that they have been trained to provide.

Nursing in Intensive Care Units

The intensive care unit (ICU) is a specialized, highly controlled environment designed to offer lifesaving and life-sustaining resources, both technological and human, to the critically ill or injured patient. Emphasis is placed on the presence of professional nurses with specific qualifications, education, and training, in a particularly rigorous staffing pattern. Often a ratio of one nurse to one patient is required to perform the necessary minute-by-minute observations, reaction, and response-and-action processes. Nurses assigned to ICUs carry immense responsibility of life and death. In larger health centers, one is likely to find nurse experts in special care units, such as coronary care, burn care, cardiac surgery care, and artificial kidney care; respiratory and stroke centers; and special nurseries.

Nursing in the Operating Room

The operating room (OR) is another specialized area of the healthcare organization that is undergoing great change. The rapid advancements in surgical diagnosis and treatment in recent years, the development and introduction of sophisticated monitoring equipment for acquiring physiologic data, and the development of other equipment and facilities are requiring new techniques, knowledge, and areas of expertise on the part of the professional nurse. The training requirements for nurses working in modern surgeries have been significantly influenced by advances in medical surgical technology.

The surgical technician continues to be a valued member of the nursing team. Under the supervision of an RN, the surgical technician assists physicians and nurses during surgical procedures and in the preparation for surgery. Although many options continue to exist in methods of training and preparing surgical technicians for their role, non-nursing personnel have demonstrated appropriate ability in response to these training programs; these programs, combined with supervised clinical practice, have somewhat alleviated the professional nursing shortages in operating rooms. The surgical technician is a health worker, well-prepared and trained by an RN who is equipped with the basic knowledge, skill, and understanding necessary to function effectively in the operating room. Nevertheless, the surgical technician must be under the direct and continuous supervision of a qualified professional nurse.

The OR nurse is a nurse clinical specialist on another, higher level. The OR nurses participate in ongoing educational programs essential to their successful utilization. With increasing emphasis and reliance on electrolyte balance, blood chemistries, antibodies, plastics, electronics, prostheses, extracorporeal circulation, organ transplantation, hyperbaric oxygenation, elaborate physiologic monitoring systems, and computers, it is obvious that the professional nurse in the operating room needs to have considerable knowledge beyond a basic understanding of the nursing curriculum.

Nursing in the Emergency Room

Each year, millions of Americans seek emergency health services. The emergency room is legally responsible for giving emergency care to anyone who requires it and should also help those with non-emergent problems by screening and making referrals as appropriate. Such a situation obviously requires around-the-clock RN staffing. One of the special staffing challenges presented to any nursing service administrator is the need to anticipate the needs of the community. For example, the location of the healthcare organization, as well as the surrounding community's psychosocial environment, will greatly determine the types and numbers of nursing personnel needed in the emergency room. In many instances, the day of the week or specific hours of the day or night will require special staffing patterns. The nurse in charge must possess a special blend of temperament, education and training, skill, and experience to meet all the problems of the emergency room. The emergency room nurse is often in a position in which independent judgment is vital—when knowing what to do first and how to get the job done is essential. The RN must teach and provide the necessary guidance to auxiliary workers, as well as help establish a harmonious and effective team relationship among physicians and nursing personnel. Calm and courteous relationships with ambulance drivers, paramedics, police, families, and the general public are also important. Legal responsibilities mean special policies and procedures that must be established in maintaining records in the emergency room. Nursing services, working closely with medical staff and administration, should also develop general policies and procedures to aid in the work of emergency room teams. The role of professional nurses in today's highly complex healthcare organizations is more significant and demanding than ever before. They must continue to be clinically competent as well as flexible and creative in their provision of nursing care.

A Look to the Future—The Changing Role of the Nurse

For years, the central leadership of healthcare organizations consisted of the medical staff, governing board, and management. Nursing management has joined this key leadership team and in the future will continue to increase in significance. The demand and necessity of reducing staffing levels as a means of containing costs places nursing management at the forefront of healthcare operations and management. Rapid organizational change, spawned by a continuing healthcare reform movement, places the nurse manager with more responsibility and accountability for governance and administrative operation.

REFERENCES

American Nurses Association. Preamble, *Code for Nurses*. Washington, DC: ANA.

Joint Commission on Accreditation of Healthcare Organizations. 1997. *Comprehensive Accreditation Manual for Hospitals: The Official Manual*. Chicago: JCAHO.

Moses, Evelyn. 1997. *The Registered Nurse Population: Findings from the National Sample Survey of Registered Nurses*. Washington, DC: DHHS, Division of Nursing.

4

Diagnostic and Therapeutic Medical Services

While diagnosis is the foundation of healthcare, therapy is its key support; therefore, efficient management of the clinical and fiscal aspects of both services reduce patient length of stay and cost, which increases net revenue for the healthcare organization. This chapter maps out the functions, procedures, and goals of the diagnostic services—clinical laboratory, radiology, nuclear medicine—and the therapeutic services—radiation therapy, occupational therapy, and physical therapy. Each diagnostic and therapeutic services' requirement for technical staff and equipment are outlined, as well as each group's relationships with other departments within the healthcare organization.

DIAGNOSTIC

Clinical Laboratory

The rapid advances in medical science are reflected in the fact that the clinical laboratory has grown much faster in recent years than have healthcare organizations in general. New and expanded outpatient procedures and sophisticated equipment have added new dimensions to the diagnosis and management of disease.

The clinical laboratory is divided into two basic sections: anatomic pathology, which deals with human tissues and includes surgical pathology, autopsy, and cytology; and clinical pathology, which deals mainly with the analysis of body fluids, principally blood, but also includes urine, gastric contents, and cerebrospinal fluid. The laboratory, while mainly interested in patient service, also expends effort in continued teaching and development to maintain a high quality of laboratory service.

Technical staff

Clinical laboratory technical staff are directed by pathologists. These are physicians with special training in anatomic pathology, clinical pathology, or both. Training generally consists of four years of residency after internship. A pathologist's medical responsibility is to interpret and report the results of the medical laboratory team to the attending physician.

If a full-time pathologist is not available, it is recommended that some part-time service be secured or that several institutions share one clinical pathologist. Laboratory specialists with PhDs provide technical help to the sections and, in many cases, have special state licensure to qualify them in specialized medical disciplines, for example, chemistry and microbiology.

The bulk of the laboratory work is carried out by licensed medical technologists. In many states, the minimal education requirement for a licensed medical technologist is four years of college with numerous required courses and one year of additional training in a clinical laboratory. The most extensive clinical laboratory training is generally provided by those laboratories approved by the American Society of Clinical Pathologists (ASCP). After completing the training, the graduate must pass an examination given by the Registry of Medical Technologists of the ASCP. Subsequent to this general licensure, subspecialty certification and training are available in blood banking, hematology, chemistry, and microbiology. In addition to medical technologists, the technical personnel in the laboratory who require specialized examinations are ctyotechnologists and histologic technicians.

Another group of specially trained personnel for laboratories are the certified laboratory assistants (CLAs). These are high-school graduates with one year of practical training in routine laboratory work. The CLA performs routine procedures under the direct supervision of a medical technologist or physician.

Other laboratory personnel include phlebotomists, secretaries, clerical personnel, and computer and data entry operators—and possibly sales, marketing, and billing employees for a reference or commercial laboratory.

Laboratory function

The principal anatomic pathology functions are performed by the pathologists, who examine tissues both in the operating room for rapid diagnosis and in the laboratory for more routine or detailed studies. They examine tissue with the naked eye, with a light microscope, and, in special cases, with an electron microscope. A large portion of the tissue examined comes from surgical specimens; autopsies are also performed, however, with the findings used to enhance medical knowledge. Fine-needle biopsy is a growing area for pathologist participation in sample collection and diagnosis. The Joint Commission has recommended that the medical staff attempt to secure autopsies for all deaths, particularly cases of unusual deaths of medical, legal, and educational interests.

Much of the work in clinical pathology is performed by medical technologists. Clinical pathologists provide clinical consultation and leadership to the laboratory. Clinical pathology is divided into subdepartments that usually include hematology, chemistry, microbiology, blood banking, and serology.

Interdepartmental relationships

The clinical laboratory service provides a major adjunct to physicians' skills in diagnosing and monitoring their patients, and depends on smooth interrelationships with other sections of the healthcare organization.

For instance, a hospitalized patient is scheduled for laboratory work by his physician. Routine laboratory work is performed on admission of the patient, either during the admission procedure or upon the patient's arrival at the unit. When the sample and the requisition stating the specific tests to be performed arrive at the laboratory, they are routed to the appropriate section for analysis.

The results are recorded and returned to the patient's chart to be reviewed by the physician. Because this information must be as timely as possible, reports are sent electronically to the nursing units in those laboratories with computer systems (or by messenger in those without). The appropriate charge for the procedure is made to the patient's account at the business office.

Information resulting from the laboratory sample requires that the clinical laboratory coordinate its daily activity with other departments such as nursing or dietary. The effects of diet and drugs on laboratory test results have been well documented; cooperation of the physician, the nurse, the dietitian, and the pharmacist is required to prevent false test results. This team should be aware of the total patient care plan as it relates to the laboratory procedures. The importance of the laboratory results as a diagnostic tool also indicates the need for coordination of the personnel involved. The test results that are brought to the physician's attention quickly and accurately enhance the organization's medical care.

Radiology

Radiology manages the use of ionizing radiation to treat disease, uses radioactive isotopes to both diagnose and treat disease, and employs fluoroscopic and radiographic x-ray equipment to diagnose disease. The medical staff of radiology is made up of physicians called radiologists, who have specialized in the use of radiant energy, radioactive isotopes, radium, cesium, and cobalt. A radiologist is qualified to use x-ray, radium, and radioactive materials for the treatment and diagnosis of disease. A radiation therapist is a radiologist who has specialized in the use of radium, cobalt, and high-voltage x-ray films only for diagnostic purposes. The department may have qualified radiologists practicing the gamut of radiology, or it may have subspecialists such as the radiation therapist, the diagnostic roentgenologist, and the nuclear medicine physician. Teaching medical centers and other large institutions may have radiologists who have specialized in vascular work, ultrasound, CT, or other emerging subspecialties.

Technical staff

The technical staff of the department may include radiologic technologists, radiation therapy technologists, nurses, and nuclear medicine technicians. Other employees include medical transcriptionists, file clerks, and a receptionist.

Under the direction of the radiologist (the department's medical director), the radiologic technologist (formerly known as x-ray technician) performs the technical radiologic procedures. Qualifications for the position are high-school graduation and completion of a formal two-year course at a school approved by the AMA. The schools, with training usually conducted by a medical school or a hospital, may be affiliated with a college or university. Additional formal training is required for a radiologic technologist to become a specialist in radiation therapy, ultrasound computer-assisted tomography, or nuclear medicine. The technologist's preparations of the patient include administering—or helping the physician administer—the proper chemical prescribed, and transferring and positioning the patient for the examination. The technologist selects, adjusts, and operates the proper radiologic equipment in accordance with established procedures. Personal contact with the patient requires that the technologist exercise prudence in words and actions.

The chief technologist is responsible for supervising the technical staff and ancillary personnel. His or her primary concern here is scheduling, work flow in the department, and the quality of the films. In directing the efforts of the technologists and supporting personnel toward maintaining high standards of technical quality and patient welfare, the chief technologist evaluates the services and coordinates the department's activities to upgrade them. The chief technologist's assignment concerning departmental, administrative, and technical activities requires additional diversified experience in radiologic technology.

In larger departments of radiology, an assistant chief technologist may be employed, reporting directly to the chief technologist in designated areas. These areas may include, among others, supervision of staff, scheduling, training programs, and safety regulations.

Many hospitals, particularly teaching institutions, have an approved school of radiologic technology, either hospital-based or in affiliation with an associate or a baccalaureate program. The school is directed by a radiologist who is assisted by a person trained at the technical level. The American Society of Radiologic Technologists has delineated the significant responsibilities of this technical director of education in coordinating the programs of a radiologic technology school. Under the direction of the radiologist, the technical director formulates and directs the staff technologists in practical application of the formal instruction.

Interdepartmental relationships

Nearly every patient admitted to the outpatient section of a hospital, or to many other healthcare organizations will, at some time during the stay, become a patient in radiology for either diagnostic or treatment purposes. Because the course of treatment that a patient's physician may wish to pursue is often dictated by the radiologic findings, this department is related to all others involved in patient care. Because its service often requires the patient's presence for long periods of time during a hospital stay, radiology is responsible for patient care during the various examining procedures. Patient areas in the department require piped-in oxygen and suction machines, as well as cardiopulmonary resuscitation equipment to handle any medical emergency when it occurs.

On completion of a radiologic examination, the physicians concerned will dictate a report of their findings from the fluoroscopic examinations they may have and from the radiographs obtained by the technical staff. These reports are distributed to the referring physicians and to medical records for entry on the patient's chart; a file copy remains with radiology. The films are also made available for purposes of consultation between the radiologist responsible for a given examination and the referring physician in charge of the patient's case. It follows, therefore, that radiology must have an area for filing the films and must work closely with medical records.

Demands of radiologic equipment on the healthcare organization

Equipment in a typical radiology room is complex and involves an apparatus to examine the internal parts of a patient. Massive equipment, often weighing nearly a ton, is suspended from the ceiling. The ceiling and floor of the area in which the x-ray equipment is installed, therefore, must have great weight-bearing capacities.

X-ray equipment makes special demands on electrical power. The transformer area that supplies all of a facility's electrical needs must have a separate section for the operation of x-ray equipment, and this section normally should not have any other electricity-consuming equipment using the same transformers.

Any room in which ionizing radiation is regularly produced requires lead lining to prevent stray radiation from leaving the room and unnecessarily exposing patients or staff to ionizing radiation. This lining creates a weight-bearing problem for the floors, and this aspect of planning requires inspection by qualified physicists and structural engineers to ensure that safety standards will be maintained.

Types of examinations

Nearly everyone is familiar with chest and extremity x-ray films and the more complex examinations of the gastrointestinal and genitourinary tract. In recent years, however, special x-ray examinations involving the vascular system have assumed an important role in diagnostic radiology. In this instance, the x-ray examining room must double as a room for minor surgery. Incisions are made, exposing arteries or veins for the insertion of catheters, which are maneuvered under fluoroscopic control into various parts of the vascular system, including the heart. Many kinds of injections are used in these examinations and all of them pose some calculated risk to the patient, much in the manner that surgery in an operating room involves a similar risk. Therefore, the special procedures section of radiology must have facilities available similar to those of operating rooms.

Diagnostic ultrasound (see Figure 4.1) has emerged as a highly technical and useful medical procedure and has been developed to examine internal structures by using high-frequency sound waves. These waves are produced by the use of a special piezoelectric crystal.

Applications for ultrasound are proliferating, especially because it is a noninvasive procedure with minimal risk to the patient. Some current applications include echocardiography to diagnose certain heart disorders, obstetric ultrasound to monitor fetal positioning and progress, gynecologic and abdominal ultrasound, neurologic testing, and ophthalmology.

Figure 4.1   Diagnostic Ultrasound

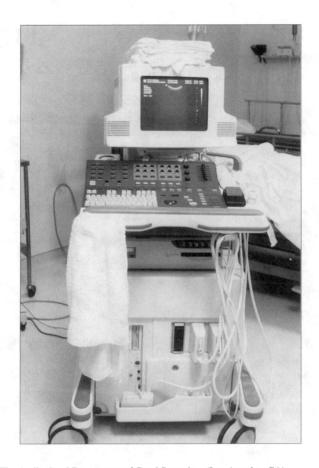

Courtesy of The Audiovisual Department of Good Samaritan (Los Angeles, CA)

Another noninvasive advancement has been the CT procedure, a technique that uses a narrow x-ray beam in a series of individual measurements at many angles. When these measurements are processed by a computer, a tomographic slice of the patient's anatomy is reconstructed. This view of a section or layer of anatomy (sometimes referred to as a CAT scan) provides a highly accurate diagnostic tool.

A revolutionary diagnostic technology is MRI, which produces detailed, cross-sectional images of the entire body noninvasively and without radiation (see Figure 4.2). It provides anatomical and biochemical information unavailable with other imaging modalities. MRI uses the harmless interaction between radio waves and hydrogen nuclei to produce signals that are

Figure 4.2   Magnetic Resonance Imaging (MRI)

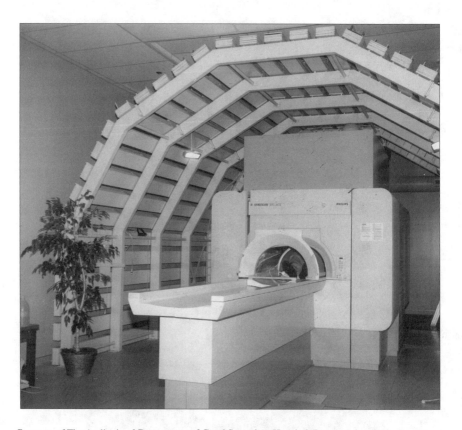

Courtesy of The Audiovisual Department of Good Samaritan Hospital (Los Angeles, CA)

converted into images by powerful computers. Because MRI uses no radiation and no routine injections of contrast materials, this painless examination is particularly useful in evaluating the central nervous system. This is
because on MRI images the bony encasement of the brain and spinal cord
does not cause the artifacts usually seen on CT scans. MRI is a superior tool
for diagnosing diseases of the brain, spine, neck, musculoskeletal system,
abdominal and pelvic area, and cardiovascular system.

Examination or treatment process

A patient's arrival in radiology for examination or treatment initiates a
series of actions, which include the following.

> 1. Radiology receives a requisition for the examination. The
>   department's records are checked to establish whether they contain

previous films of the patient. If he or she has been examined previously, the old films are obtained from the film file area and attached to the requisition. If not, the patient's name, number, and other pertinent information are entered on the face of a new film jacket.

2. Nursing personnel, radiology personnel, or the centralized transportation pool may transport the patient to the radiology department. The patient arrives at the receptionist's desk with a doctor's order for a particular examination. The nurse will have prepared the patient with the diet required or medication prescribed for the radiologic procedure.

3. The patient is then assigned to the technician who will handle the examination.

4. After the patient has completed the examination, the films are passed through a high-speed processor for development and drying. Modern processing takes only 90 seconds.

5. The examination results are checked, and the patient is then discharged from the department.

Nuclear Medicine

Nuclear medicine involves applying small amounts of short-lived radioactive tracers for the treatment of patients, although it is employed predominantly for diagnostic or prognostic purposes. Using the basic mathematics and physics of tracer methodology, nuclear medicine methods are widely established in clinical medicine; most authorities, however, agree that they have only begun to scratch the surface in terms of nuclear medicine's potential capabilities.

Patient diagnostic procedures require introduction of a radioactive tracer by various means, most often by intravenous injection. The particular tracer is selected for both its physiologic and physical characteristics so that both the function and the anatomy of the organ system under evaluation can be properly studied. The resulting emitted rays are detected by sensitive crystals in increasingly complex machines that are capable of rapid sequential imaging as well as tomographic imaging and graphic representation of the tracer's distribution. In addition, through the use of extremely sophisticated computers, quantitative functional information on such organs as the heart and kidney can be obtained in a safe, simple, noninvasive manner. These nuclear medicine procedures differ from x-ray procedures primarily in that the latter use rays transmitted through the patient, resulting in images that give more anatomic but less functional information than do the nuclear medicine procedures. Laboratory in vitro nuclear medicine procedures use radioactive materials in analyzing specimens obtained from patients; radioimmunoassay (identifying substances radioactively through their capacity to act as antigens) is an important and rapidly expanding part of nuclear medicine.

Technical staff

The nuclear medicine staff is headed by a nuclear medicine physician with postgraduate training, which requires two years in nuclear medicine and two years in diagnostic radiology, internal medicine, or pathology for eligibility in the American Board of Nuclear Medicine. Certification as a nuclear medicine technologist requires one year of training, combining didactic and practical experience; a prerequisite is high school graduation. Training of both physicians and technologists is an important function of the nuclear medicine department.

Examination process

Nuclear medicine procedures are handled as follows:

1. The attending physician's request for nuclear medicine service is forwarded by telephone, pneumatic tube, or computer to the nuclear medicine department as soon as is feasible after the order is given. As much background information as possible should be given to the nuclear medicine physician so that he or she may be certain that the optimal procedure is performed to best answer the clinical questions.

2. Routine requests are promptly scheduled and patient unit personnel advised of the appointment time. Depending on the specific diagnostic test and the condition of the patient, the radiotracer dose may be given either on the unit or in the nuclear medicine department.

3. Some tests are started immediately following tracer injection, while others require a waiting period of 20 minutes, an hour, or sometimes several days. Each patient is assigned to a technologist who explains the procedure, ensures that it is completed properly, and has primary responsibility. However, no patient leaves the department until all the views necessary as determined by the nuclear medicine physician are completed. While in the department, the patient is observed by either a technologist or a nurse, and a physician is available even though radioactive materials have no pharmacologic effect and allergic reactions are extremely rare.

4. Once started, procedures generally are completed and the patient is ready to return to the floor within 15 to 60 minutes. However, the patient often is required to return for "delayed" studies after several hours or days.

5. Results generally are known within a few minutes and are written by the nuclear medicine physician in the patient's progress chart. Sometimes, further computer analysis or lengthy interpretive evaluation

is required, and results—when determined—are telephoned to the attending physician.

6. The final report is then promptly dictated, typed, and sent directly to the patient unit; it should be available in the patient's chart either the same day or the next working day following completion of the examination. A copy should be mailed to the referring physician by nuclear medicine or medical records as soon as possible.

A nuclear medicine physician is always available for consultation with attending and house staff physicians before studies are performed, to plan the procedure optimally, and after the studies are completed. All nuclear medicine procedures can be performed on a full spectrum of patients— outpatients, transportable inpatients, or, if necessary, bedridden inpatients using special portable cameras at the bedside.

THERAPEUTIC

Radiation Therapy

Radiation therapy uses high-energy x-rays, cobalt, electrons, and other sources of radiation to treat human diseases, especially cancer. According to current practice, radiation therapy is used alone or in combination with surgery or chemotherapy (drugs). In addition to external beam therapy, radioactive implants, as well as therapy performed with heat (hyperthermia) are available.

Technical staff

The radiation therapist is a physician who has had several years of additional training in the use of radiation in the treatment of disease. The physician has acquired special knowledge in evaluating patients with cancer and in the use of radiation-producing substances for treatment.

Among the many professionally educated persons aiding the radiation therapist is the radiation physicist who has extensive training in the planning of treatments designed to deliver the desired doses of radiation. The dosimetrist assists the physician and physicist in calculating the treatment. The radiation therapy technologist, who has been trained in a certified school of radiologic technology and has additional training and experience in radiation therapy, is responsible for administering the calculated doses under the supervision of the physician.

The radiation therapy department may also employ a nurse with a particular interest and training in the care of radiation therapy patients. Ancillary personnel for transportation, secretarial services, and logistics make up much of the remainder of the staff. The ability to computerize many of the treatment activities has stimulated the development of various levels of computer expertise within virtually all radiation therapy departments.

Types of equipment

One or more different machines may be used in the course of treatment. These include x-ray machines, linear accelerators (see Figure 4.3), a betatron, and for modern treatment of brain tumors, the gamma knife (see Figure 4.4). The equipment used in radiation therapy presents a greater problem than those employed in diagnostic radiology because the equipment exposes patient and employees to unnecessary, very-high-energy irradiation. The rooms containing the equipment require extra concrete protection, which will prevent extraneous radiation leakage, and the foundations must be capable of bearing the weight of both the lead lining and the massive equipment.

Patient referral

The patient is usually referred to the radiation therapist by another physician for an opinion on whether the patient's condition will improve through

Figure 4.3   Linear Accelerator

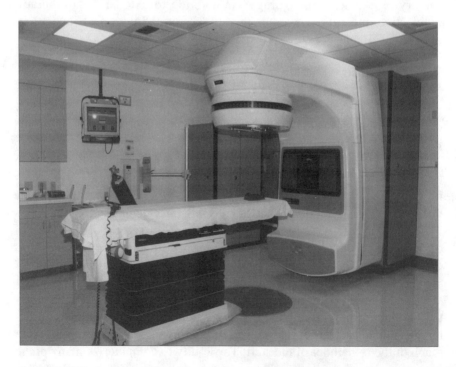

Courtesy of The Audiovisual Department of Good Samaritan Hospital (Los Angeles, CA)

Figure 4.4   The Gamma Knife

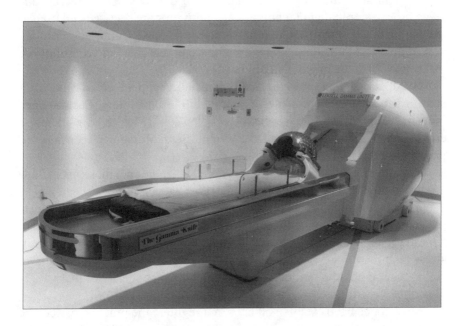

Courtesy of The Audiovisual Department of Good Samaritan Hospital (Los Angeles, CA)

radiation treatments. This involves a thorough physical examination, x-ray films and pathology slides, and a review of previous medical records; it may also require additional special examinations. If it is decided that radiation could be useful as a treatment modality, the anatomic location is determined, calculations are made for delivering the appropriate amount of radiation to the exact site, and the schedule is specified. Following the course of treatment, a complete report is sent to the patient's referring doctor.

Occupational Therapy

Occupational therapy is the therapeutic use of work and play activities that increase independent function, enhance development, and prevent disability. The activities may involve the adaptation of tasks or the environment to achieve maximum independence and to enhance quality of life.

Diagnoses within the realm of occupational therapy intervention include developmental deficits, birth defects, learning disabilities, traumatic injury, burns, neurological conditions, orthopedic conditions, mental deficiencies, and emotional disorders. Within the healthcare system, occupational therapy plays various roles including promoting health, preventing disability, developing or restoring of functional capacity, guiding adaptation within physical and mental parameters, and teaching creative problem solving to increase independent function. Providing occupational therapy services begins with an evaluation of the patient and the selection of therapeutic goals. Specific treatment techniques and activities are selected and used as a dynamic therapist–patient relationship is developed. Continual reevaluation of progress and communication with other members of the healthcare team assist in the achievement of goals.

Occupational therapy is medically directed treatment and may be available in acute care hospitals, clinics, rehabilitation centers, business and industry, home health care services, school systems, sheltered workshops, correctional institutions, extended care facilities, community agencies, and private practices.

Requirements for becoming a registered occupational therapist include graduation from an accredited program with a bachelor of science degree in occupational therapy, a bachelor's degree in a related field plus a certificate in occupational therapy or an entry-level master's degree, or completion of a master's degree in occupational therapy. Following completion of study, six to nine months of field work in adult or pediatric physical disabilities and in mental health are required to obtain clinical experience in a variety of healthcare settings.

Most states have established laws that regulate the practice of occupational therapy. Registered occupational therapists must also meet specific state licensing requirements to be eligible to practice within the state.

Preparation for becoming a certified occupational therapy assistant includes college study at an accredited institution, leading to an associate's degree in occupational therapy. Field work for a certified occupational therapy assistant is two months.

Following the completion of an approved program and field work, candidates must pass the national certification examination issued by the American Occupational Therapy Association. Some states have also established licensing requirements for certified occupational therapy assistants.

Opportunities are now available at some universities to obtain master's degrees and doctorates in occupational therapy.

Physical Therapy

Physical medicine and rehabilitation have expanded into many areas of medical specialties. Physical therapy can be applied in most disciplines of medicine: neurology, neurosurgery, orthopedics, general surgery, family practice, pediatrics, geriatrics, obstetrics, rheumatology, internal medicine, cardiovascular medicine, cardiopulmonary medicine, psychiatry, sports medicine, burn and wound care, chronic pain management, and community health education.

Medical rehabilitation must involve the entire healthcare team—the physician, nurse, social worker, occupational therapists, other physical therapists, and other closely allied personnel. The objective is either to eliminate the patient's disability or to alleviate as fully as possible the patient's mental, social, or physical abilities impaired by disease or injury. The primary purpose of physical therapy in rehabilitation is to promote optimal health and function by applying scientific principles and treatment modalities as therapeutic exercise, heat, low-energy laser, cold, water, therapeutic massage, electricity, ultrasound, and biofeedback (see Figure 4.5).

Technical staff

The physical therapist is a professional trained in methods of physical medicine and who performs physical therapy evaluations, identifies treatment goals, and implements treatment programs designed to meet individual needs, goals, and abilities. A physical therapist's formal education may consist of a four-year college bachelor's degree with an emphasis on biological and medical sciences, a twelve-month certificate course for students with a bachelor's degree, or graduate training leading to a master's degree in physical therapy. The American Physical Therapy Association has recently raised entry-level education of physical therapists to a postbaccalaureate degree. In addition to academic training, all programs include at least six months of supervised clinical practice. The practice of physical therapy is regulated by state law, and state licensure, or registration, legally represents the professional right to practice.

The physical therapist assistant is a skilled technical health worker who, under the direct supervision of a physical therapist, assists in the patient's treatment program. Training consists of a two-year junior college or community college program leading to an associate's degree. Some states require licensure or registration to practice as a physical therapist assistant.

Physical therapy aides with proper training and close supervision may be used to assist the professional staff in various aspects of patient care or departmental activities. Clerical staff are needed to perform tasks related to patient scheduling, record keeping, and correspondence.

Facilities and equipment

The amount of equipment and space needed varies with the extent of the physical medicine program and the types of patient referred for physical therapy. Common modalities used include hot packs, ice packs, paraffin baths, hydrotherapy with whirlpools or a therapeutic pool, diathermy, ultrasound, massage, electrical stimulation, spinal traction, biofeedback, and low-energy laser (see Figure 4.5)

Figure 4.5   Physical Therapy Equipment

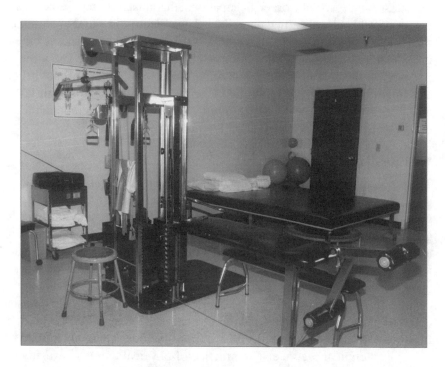

Courtesy of The Audiovisual Department of Good Samaritan Hospital (Los Angeles, CA)

Therapeutic exercise, joint and soft-tissue mobilization, and neuromuscular reeducation are techniques used to reduce pain; improve range of motion; and increase strength, endurance, and coordination to achieve optimal function. Other procedures include training patients in the use of orthotic and prosthetic devices and other assistive devices, including crutches, canes, and wheelchairs.

A Look to the Future

The managed care system has had the effect of shorter length of stay and increased outpatient utilization in most healthcare organizations. As a result, cost-containment initiatives are targeted in such large outpatient diagnostic service areas as clinical laboratory and radiology. Because the supplies and equipment used to perform sophisticated and much-needed diagnostic procedures are very expensive, these health service departments are targeted as high-potential areas to reduce the cost of providing services. Cooperative utilization of expensive radiology equipment between neighboring health service entities and shared purchase agreements between health service providers are examples of current and potential cost-containment measures. Outpatient diagnostic and therapeutic health service volume will continue to increase in the future as more and more pressure is placed on healthcare organizations to shorten the length of stay.

Clinical and Support Services

Although a healthcare organization is known primarily for its provision of medical and psychological treatment, it cannot deliver comprehensive, quality healthcare to its patients and a safe environment to its staff without the aid of ancillary units, such as the pharmacy, food and nutrition service, social work and patient advocacy, environmental services, purchasing, and engineering and plant operation. These support services are not only identified in this chapter, their interdepartmental function, relationship, and importance are discussed as well.

PHARMACY SERVICES

As healthcare organization services and medical sciences continue to expand dramatically in today's managed care environment, the practice of pharmacy has been developing in scope and complexity as well. The pharmacist has combined expertise in the fields of medications and medication systems to become a valued member of the healthcare team.

Qualifications of the Pharmacist

Pharmacists spend a minimum of five years on professional education after completing high school. After graduation from an accredited school of pharmacy, they may complete an additional year of practical experience in a pharmacy residency program. Approximately one-third of all graduates have a six-year doctor of pharmacy degree. Although many disciplines are used in the pharmacist's daily responsibilities, specialized training is essential in both the professional and administrative areas.

As a type of nonphysician, the pharmacist dispenses drugs upon receiving a prescription from a physician. Many are not aware that the pharmacist is involved with members of the medical team as a primary consultant on drug therapy. A diverse professional background is needed for the pharmacist to correlate the actions of drugs with interactive items, such as the patient's diet, laboratory tests, other medications, and health status.

Organizational Relationship to the Medical Staff

The Joint Commission requires a collaborative, interdisciplinary approach to administering medications. In practice, this means that the pharmacists and medical staff members meet regularly to review appropriateness of medication orders and administration to the patient. This committee, commonly referred to as the Pharmacy and Therapeutics Committee, develops a formulary and monitors medication use and other therapeutic policies. Although not mandatory, the Joint Commission has recommended that healthcare organizations have such a committee. A nursing representative and administrative officer may also be included to achieve a broader resource base on this committee.

The committee serves as an advisory body to the medical staff and administration on matters pertinent to medication procedures. A related function of the committee is the development of programs to disseminate the latest medication information to the medical and paramedical staffs.

The Hospital Formulary

One of the recommended responsibilities of the pharmacy and therapeutics committee is the preparation and continual revision of the hospital formulary. By definition of the American Society of Hospital Pharmacists (1964), "The hospital formulary is a continually revised compilation of pharmaceuticals which reflects the current clinical judgment of the medical staff."

The formulary provides a listing of drugs, usually by their generic or nonproprietary name. This is supplemented with pertinent information about the products. If some form of physicians' consent to a formulary system has been given, the formulary allows the pharmacist to fill the prescription with the generic-equivalent medication that, in his or her professional judgment, meets the therapeutic requirements. The advantage is that unnecessary duplication in purchasing, storing, and dispensing of drugs can be avoided.

Dispensing Medications to Inpatients

Prescriptions originating for patients within the healthcare organization are to be filled only in the pharmacy (see Figure 5.1). The physician writes the medication order for the patient.

The order is transferred to the pharmacy by nursing personnel, pharmacy personnel, or a central transportation service. Electronic data processing equipment can be used to transmit the order and, at the same time, to update the patient's medical record, the pharmacy inventory, and medication profiles, as well as place the charge on the patient's bill.

The pharmacist receives the drug requisition and checks it for possible errors, omissions, or incompatibilities. If any clarification is needed, the

Figure 5.1 Medication Preparation

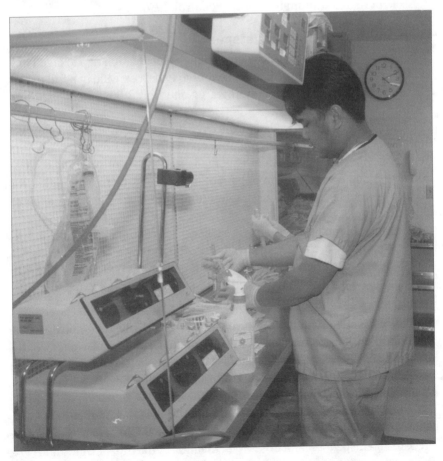

Courtesy of The Audiovisual Department of Good Samaritan Hospital (Los Angeles, CA)

pharmacist communicates with the attending physician or nurse. The medication is selected and checked against the requisition, then labeled and checked a second time against the requisition. The pharmacy technician may do some of the prepackaging and labeling under supervision, but the final responsibility for the drug and its labeling lies with the pharmacist.

The medication is transported back to the nursing station for administration to the patient by the nurse. The charge is made to the patient's account, and the pharmacy inventory is adjusted, which completes the medication dispensing process.

Floor stock medications

A number of emergency drugs and widely used drugs and medications may be kept on the patient units as floor stock items. Although this eliminates much of the handling and paperwork of the prescription system, the quantity is kept to a minimum to properly control the drugs.

Medication distribution systems

Unit-dose dispensing. Unit-dose dispensing is medication in packaged individual-dose units, or units of use. The unit may be a capsule in a foil packet, one injection in a disposable syringe, or one liquid dose in a disposable bottle.

The system has many advantages over floor stock or standard prescription packaging and is strongly recommended by health services accreditation agencies. One important advantage is that the identity of the medication is retained up to the point of patient intake. Nursing time benefits from the positive identification, contamination-free packaging, and accurate labeling.

Because all medications are prepackaged and completely identified, the medication order can be filled by a trained pharmacy technician under the supervision of the pharmacist. This method promotes better use of time for the highly trained pharmacist, which allows him or her to function more effectively as the drug therapy consultant on the medical team.

Satellite pharmacy. Although unit-dose dispensing can be accomplished from the central pharmacy location, the decentralized satellite pharmacy continues to receive increased consideration. The satellite is a completely equipped medication room in a patient unit staffed by a pharmacist and possibly a technician during a specified portion of the day.

These pharmacy rooms provide more efficient control of patient medications, and they save valuable nursing time. The pharmacist is available to prepare and dispense a unit dose of medication at the proper time and is also there to consult with the doctor or nurse on special situations concerning drug therapy. An intravenous (IV) additive program, in which the pharmacist prepares the solutions with the prescribed drug additives, can also be incorporated into the satellite pharmacy, although many hospitals with decentralized systems keep the IV preparations centralized for economy. The Joint Commission organizes the establishment of intravenous additive services in healthcare organizations.

An important result of having the pharmacist in the patient area has been the development of a patient-oriented rather than a product-oriented health professional. In the satellite situation, a patient medication profile is usually prepared on all medications each patient is taking. This profile provides the vital information the pharmacist needs for proper monitoring of the patient's drug therapy.

Clinical Pharmacy

Clinical pharmacy continues to be an increasingly common area of pharmacy practice. *Clinical* implies the practice of pharmacy in the presence of patients, whether they are hospitalized or are ambulatory outpatients visiting a clinic or community health center. Obviously, the term does not imply that this practice should be confined to the institutional setting; the institution is, however, the ideal training ground for the clinical practice of pharmacy.

Three basic components of the clinical role in the practice of pharmacy have been defined:

1. communication (with patients, physicians, nurses);
2. counseling (primarily for patients, but also for healthcare team members); and
3. consulting (supplying detailed drug information).

Information obtained in the institutional setting can be applied to any area of pharmacy practice because the most important aspect of clinical exposure is contact with patients. Thus, this setting enables the patient to become the point of application of acquired knowledge.

Pharmaceutical Manufacturing

The majority of all solid drugs are commercially packaged by pharmaceutical companies in unit-dose form, leaving the minority of drugs to be packaged by the healthcare organization for a unit-dose program. The manufacturing section of the pharmacy is organized to prepare the various forms of drugs for packaging that meet the specialized requirements of a pharmacy program. Pharmaceutical manufacturing includes preparing and repackaging solid and liquid drug forms and injectable medications in disposable syringes. Specialized equipment and quality control are key considerations to emphasize in developing the pharmaceutical manufacturing area. Depending on the services needed by the staff, the scope may range from repackaging medications to preparing solutions for intravenous administration.

Radiopharmacy

The concept of pharmacists needing to know about radioactivity is not new. Pharmaceutical manufacturers began marketing radioactive pharmaceuticals in 1948, and shortly thereafter, the vice chairman of the Joint Committee on Atomic Energy of Congress suggested that atomic energy should be a matter of major concern to practicing pharmacists. At the same time, a professor of pharmaceutical chemistry stated unequivocally that the hospital-based pharmacist should be prepared to provide information and assistance to hospitals undertaking radioisotope programs and should, in many instances, take the initiative in the establishment of facilities that would use these materials in medical practice and research.

The functions of a radiopharmaceutical service (giving some indication of the benefits that may accrue to the hospital that supports such an operation) may be summarized as formulation, control, research and development, and consultation. A course, or courses, in radiopharmacy is, therefore, rapidly becoming essential in the coursework of the undergraduate pharmacy major, and a number of schools of pharmacy currently offer instruction on radiopharmaceutical topics both at the undergraduate and the graduate level.

If future developments in the use of radionuclides in diagnostic and therapeutic applications are to continue, there will be a continuing and expanding need for expert radiopharmacist/radiopharmaceutical capability on hospital staff throughout the nation.

Dispensing Medications to Outpatients

The area in a hospital for dispensing drugs to outpatients can be within the central pharmacy or located separately to provide better public access. The dispensing routine can be compared to the operation of a community pharmacy. The physician gives the patient a written prescription, which is filled by the pharmacy staff. The medication given to the patient by the pharmacist is usually accompanied by a written and/or verbal instruction on its use, by which the patient must comply. Compliance is a patient's adherence to a physician's prescribed therapy and noncompliance is nonadherence to a prescribed therapy. Patients' recovery or health outcome depends, to a large extent, on their compliance with the physician's directions regarding their prescribed drug therapy.

The physician or one of the physician's agents—for example, the pharmacist or nurse—must communicate prescribed therapy to the patient or to the patient's spouse, parent, or friend. The probable outcome of such an encounter is that the physician prescribes therapy and expects the patient to adhere to it, whereas the patient either adheres to or does not adhere to that prescribed therapy.

Because pharmacists are involved with dispensing medications, with appropriate written or verbal directions or both, dispensing refills of these same medications, and are in contact with patients at time of admission, discharge, and clinic revisits, they are ideally placed to monitor individual patient compliance patterns. It is incumbent on pharmacists, therefore, to apply their knowledge and experience routinely and consistently, along with communicating with patients and counseling them, to assist in redirecting noncompliant patient behavior, which appears to be more prevalent over time than does compliant behavior.

Pharmacy Administration

Operating the pharmacy departments is the direct responsibility of the chief pharmacist or director of pharmacy services, who is responsible to the administrator of the institution. Larger institutions may have an assistant chief pharmacist for the inpatient, outpatient, and manufacturing areas. For smaller institutions unable to obtain the services of a pharmacist on a full-time basis, the Joint Commission recommends that they obtain the consultant services of either a healthcare pharmacist or a community pharmacist to supervise the policies and procedures of the department.

In addition to pharmacists, the pharmacy staff may include technicians, clerical staff, and storeroom personnel. The technicians can be specially trained for a wide range of tasks, from manufacturing to part of the dispensing process. The increasingly flexible technician's job has begun to relieve the pharmacist of many manual tasks, resulting in better utilization of pharmacists.

Pharmacy Technology and Automation

Technology and automation will continue to affect the pharmaceutical profession. Future pharmacy computer systems will help pharmacists assess patients' medication needs, evaluate drug therapy, and manage patient information. Advanced systems are being developed for automatic dispensing and for distributing medications from nurses' stations in healthcare organizations, including long-term care facilities. Bar codes are being used in medication dispensing, verifying prescriptions, selecting patient brochures, and screening for drug interactions. Pharmacies in the future will rely on information networks to store, manage, and communicate patient information.

A Look to the Future

The traditional role of the pharmacist in a healthcare organization has included some managerial functions, including central supply and purchasing. A role that continues to expand is that of "clinical pharmacist," with the responsibility for prescribing drugs, dispensing and administering drugs, documenting professional activities, directing patient involvement, and reviewing drug utilization. The role of the clinical pharmacist will continue to expand within the managed care environment to include dispensing drugs and advising patients at bedside, consulting actively with physicians, and monitoring drug therapy. All of these pharmacy activities along the continuum of care in healthcare organizations are intended to enhance quality of care and reduce costs. This will continue to be the focus of the health reform agenda in years to come. Pharmacy services account for a significant percentage of operating costs, which have inflated substantially over the years. As a result, this service is—and will continue to be—the target of much-needed cost-containment efforts.

SOCIAL SERVICES

As there is deeper insight into the outside influences affecting the patient's security and well-being—particularly social, economic, and environmental conditions—appreciation for the role that medical social worker can perform has also become greater. Social service focuses on three areas: the patient, the medical team, and the community. For the patient, the objectives are to remove environmental and emotional obstacles that may jeopardize recovery and to help the patient, and his or her family, adjust to the complex circumstances precipitated by the medical situation. The medical social worker, an essential member of the healthcare team, gathers and interprets pertinent information about the patient's social and emotional status and the patient's pattern of adjustment.

Staff

Personnel of the social services department have extensive knowledge of the community and can make use of appropriate agencies for the purpose of complete physical and psychologic rehabilitation of the patient; with the smooth transition from an acute condition to healthy status, a more comprehensive recovery may be achieved.

In healthcare organizations where the potential of social services is understood, social services is organized on a departmental level, with the director of social service reporting to a member of administration of the institution. Becoming a medical social worker—an expert in understanding human relations—requires years of formal education and sensitivity to a variety of cultural backgrounds and situations. To qualify as a medical social worker, one must obtain a master's degree from a graduate school of social work accredited by the Council on Social Work Education. An undergraduate background in the liberal arts is a preferred prerequisite. A bachelor's degree in social work is also available, and personnel with this background generally focus on the patient's discharge planning needs.

Because of periodic shortages of professionally trained personnel, some college graduates are being trained to accept some social service duties of social work assistants.

A specialist in helping patients who are suffering mental or emotional disturbances is called the psychiatric social worker. This professional's objectives are similar to those of the medical social worker, although the required training in the field of mental health is more intensive. Because of the levels of training available in schools of social work, social workers are increasingly becoming qualified to provide individual and group psychotherapy.

Interdepartmental Relationships

Because the patient's physical recovery often involves a comparatively healthy psychological state, which means easing social pressure as well as inner stress, the social worker is an integral part of the healthcare team under the direction of the attending physician. A request for individual social casework may be initiated by a physician or by other personnel in the organization, such as those in the admitting department or physical therapy. The attending physician should be informed of these other referrals.

Some of the social service department's activities are related to the patient's financial status. This information may be of value to the business office in establishing the patient's payment plan.

As the physician deals with physical disease, the social worker discusses with the patient the other problems that may prevent a speedy and thorough recovery, or factors that might include housing, finances, family, and emotional and psychological distress. Through his or her extensive knowledge of the community's resources, the social worker can help alleviate these problems and, thus, can contribute profoundly to the patient's total rehabilitation.

A patient's family is often in need of as much help as the patient. The illness of one member of a closely knit family can cause deep emotional problems in other family members; similarly, the attitude of family members can greatly affect the patient's progress in recovering. Therefore, the social worker does not treat the patient alone but rather the family as a unit for the purpose of the patient's speedy and thorough recovery.

A Look to the Future

In the future, social work professionals in healthcare will need to adapt dramatically to meet the needs of individuals and their families as the system of care changes from an acute care focus to a community-based focus and as individuals seek more active participation in their own care decisions.

PATIENT ADVOCATE

The patient advocate promotes patient's rights, and the emphasis is on healthcare from the patient's perspective. Some of the patient advocate's functions include explaining and describing medical and surgical procedures for the patient, working directly with the patient and family, responding to their questions and complaints, helping with living wills, and discussing medical options. The advocate interacts with the facility management, healthcare providers, and community agencies to meet the needs of patients and their families.

HEALTH SCIENCES LIBRARY

In recent years, the volume of medical and scientific data has reached unmanageable proportions, and continuing an in-service education has become a standard of quality (in some professions, a requirement for relicensure). One result has been the emergence of the healthcare institution as a vital educational resource for the healthcare practitioner, researcher, and student, and for the community itself.

Within each institution the health sciences library is the information center for institutional activity. The traditional image of the library as being merely a collection of books and magazines has been replaced by a dynamic, service-oriented department providing much-needed comprehensive services.

Staff

The informational and educational needs of a particular organization determine the staffing level of the library. An institution with a large education or research facility will generally employ a qualified medical librarian, who is usually a graduate of a library school accredited by the American Library Association, certified by the Medical Library Association, or who has the equivalent in experience and training. If it is unnecessary to employ an individual that is highly qualified, or if a qualified medical librarian is unavailable, consulting services are often obtained to ensure the excellence and effectiveness of the library services. These services are available on an area or regional basis. The other individuals employed by the library are usually specifically trained to perform basic library service functions, including ordering, cataloging, organizing, and circulating library materials.

Services

The value of the health sciences library lies not in the "warehousing" of medical and scientific literature but in providing ease of accessibility and delivery of essential information to the library user. The library maintains a core of pertinent books, journals, and reference materials for convenient and immediate use. An arrangement will also be in place for obtaining interlibrary loans either from neighboring sources or from regional library networks. Other types of library services should include providing reference services by the library staff, which include lists of articles or books on specific subjects or short answers to specific questions; verifying citations in the literature; and maintaining a convenient method of photocopying. The extent to which the health sciences library is able to keep its users aware of its presence and worth—and to represent the educational and research interests of the many students, teachers, and healthcare practitioners who require its services—is the measure of a useful and successful library resource.

The basic role of the health sciences librarian has not changed significantly over the years. What *has* changed is the environment in which this role is carried out and the tools used to accomplish it. The ever-changing healthcare system will require a continual review of specialty healthcare education and the use of emerging technologies in delivering timely and efficient health science library services.

Changes in the health information environment will continue to present major challenges to health sciences librarians. To meet these challenges—not the least of which is technological advances in library service delivery—librarians must initiate informal, self-directed, lifelong learning to their careers.

FOOD AND NUTRITIONAL SERVICES

Optimal nutrition is one of the cornerstones of good health, and providing the diet that best meets the patient's needs is therefore an essential element of medical treatment. The patient's nutritional state is enhanced with medically sound diet prescriptions, regular patient monitoring, and palatable, culturally sensitive (and sensible) foods. Inadequate nutrition has been shown to contribute to length of patient stay and to a less-than-acceptable patient outcome. The primary function of food and nutritional services is to provide each patient with high-quality nutrition that meets individual needs during the patient's hospital stay.

Staff

Food and nutritional services departments can be structured very differently based on needs of the individual organization. The director is ultimately responsible for all food services activities and, depending on the organization's size, may have supervisors covering different areas of responsibility.

Although in the past, it was almost expected that a registered dietitian would be the department director, this is no longer necessarily the case. The director may be an experienced food service manager who has gained expertise from practice and management in other healthcare facilities, restaurants, or hotel kitchens. This arrangement is well accepted under Joint Commission standards, provided the clinical area is assigned a chief clinical dietitian to oversee all direct patient care activities.

The food service director is usually a key player in many hospital activities and spends some time away from the department. As a result, he or she usually depends heavily on subordinates to manage the daily operations. The director, however, is ultimately responsible for fulfilling all department budgetary, service, and regulatory requirements while maintaining high employee morale. Some departments have an assistant director who assumes responsibility in the director's absence.

It is not uncommon to find restaurant-trained chefs overseeing all kitchen activities, including the patient tray line, cafeteria meal service, physician meals, and catering. The chef or kitchen supervisor is responsible for purchasing food and supplies, ensuring cost and quality controls, maintaining acceptable levels of sanitation, and supervising all kitchen employees.

The cafeteria will be supervised, ideally, by someone very knowledgeable and creative regarding food and its salability, as hospitals look more toward the cafeteria as a revenue-generating area with sales potential. Many larger organizations have contracts with fast-food establishments and find the arrangement to be quite popular and profitable.

The clinical dietitians are responsible for assuring each patient's high nutritional status and for developing each specific care plan. The clinical dietitian communicates this information to medical staff and to other interdisciplinary team members. Clinical dietitians monitor individual nutritional progress, diet acceptance, food quality, portion control, and accuracy of the diets prescribed. Ongoing quality assurance studies are performed to determine that food and nutritional services are provided with the right level of consistency.

Dietitians also work in teaching research capacities. Outpatient nutritional education and community outreach programs are offered at many hospitals. Medical staff and students may take classes in nutrition from hospital-based clinical dietitians. Research-oriented teaching facilities often require the services of clinical dietitians for studies. A dietitian attends a four-year college program and must spend an additional year affiliated with a facility approved by the American Dietetic Association (ADA) to become a member of the ADA and to be eligible for a registration examination. Those who successfully complete the examination are then considered registered dietitians.

The remainder of the food service staff—the majority—are those concerned with the clerical functions and those engaged in actual preparation. In addition to the general secretarial and clerical duties found in most departments, the dietary clerical worker's duties include tallying patient menu items, processing computerized diet orders, and checking the actual tray-line process for accuracy. The food service workers themselves cover the whole range of food preparation—storage, actual preparation, cooking tray assembly, serving, and clean-up activities. Each position is important in maintaining the highest institutional standards of food preparation and services.

Equipment and Facilities

By design, dietary departments range widely in physical layouts and equipment. The ideal arrangement should facilitate the task of food purchasing, receiving and storage, refrigeration, preparation, delivery, and disposal while still maintaining product quality. The amount of space required for each duty will vary from one institution to the next. Generally, separate work areas are designed for receiving and storage, food preparation, tray assembly, dishwashing, and waste disposal. Depending on the institution, there may also be a cafeteria, a physicians' dining room, and a small service kitchen located next to the institution's conference rooms.

Food Distribution

Because the food must be brought to the patient, its efficient distribution must be well planned. One of the more popular systems currently used is the pellet system. Metal bases, filled with either wax or metal pellets, are heated prior to meal distribution. The meal is served on a heated plate, which is set on the hot metal base. A heavy plastic lid, preferably insulated, covers the meal to assist in the heat retention. Once the trays are prepared in the kitchen, they are placed on a cart and delivered to a specific floor. The pellet system is very effective in slowing heat loss, but the key to providing a meal where hot food is hot and cold food is cold also includes timely tray delivery to the patient once the food has been delivered to the nursing unit. The responsibility for serving the trays to the patients may fall upon food service staff, nurses, nursing aides, or volunteers.

Another, less-used meal distribution system includes hot and cold food trucks, where prepared food is placed into the heated or cooled portion of the cart and transported to the nursing unit to be served. Still another system includes use of precooked foods prepared by microwave on the nursing units before being served to the patients.

Interdepartmental Relationships

Food and nutritional services must work closely with many departments, but it depends most heavily on the nursing staff for accurate patient information. In accordance with the prescribed treatment for their patients, physicians order diets much as if they were ordering drugs or nursing care. The nursing staff or unit managers then notify the dietary department.

Keeping track of extra meals can save money. Under many situations in the hospital, patients may not eat: They may be in surgery, they may be undergoing laboratory tests, they may be in the x-ray department, and so on. Food and nutritional services must know this to plan accordingly. Perhaps the patient needs a late meal, after the regular meals have been served. This requires the coordination of physicians, nursing staff, and dietary department. If the time of the patient's discharge or transfer is noted carefully in the dietary department, there will be less inefficiency in preparing too many meals or in delivering meals to the wrong floor.

Reaction to medication has been known to affect a patient's sense of taste, a difficulty that may compound the problem effect of having to eat modified food. Finally, much care should be given to make the menu inclusive and tempting, and the service and tray as attractive as possible.

In response to the managed care healthcare environment, dietitians in the future will need to review practice opportunities in new and different settings and to develop additional skills to make a successful transition. The shift in healthcare financing from fee-for-service to a capitated system continues to have a significant impact on the profession.

ENVIRONMENTAL SERVICES

The Joint Commission has outlined a series of functional standards specific to the management of the environment of care. The goal of this function is "to provide a safe, functional, and effective environment for patients, staff members, and other individuals" in the healthcare setting. Environmental services (formerly called housekeeping) in a healthcare organization is directly involved in achieving this performance standard. Both medical and administrative personnel are frequently misled by the seemingly similar tasks performed by family members in the average home and by environmental services employees in the healthcare organization. Both at home and in healthcare organizations, windows and walls are washed, and general cleaning, mopping, removal of trash, and other seemingly domestic duties are performed. In actual performance, these tasks may not be similar at all.

Environmental services employees often use highly sophisticated equipment, caustic chemicals, and complicated techniques when performing interior environmental work. These professionals must be trained to perform their functions on a level far beyond the householder's imagination—that is, in the intensiveness and extensiveness of germ control, in the general control of infection, and in the unique requirements and risks inherent in working with isolated, infectious patients and a variety of hazardous materials.

While interior decor of hospital rooms and buildings must be designed with the functions of the internal environmental service in mind, it must be easy to clean, flexible, and safe.

The importance of good environmental standards in a healthcare organization cannot be measured simply by the amount of money spent. Adherence to these standards is important not only for patient morale and well-being but also for employee safety and invaluable public relations. The average administrator probably receives more comments, good or bad, about the environmental service than about any other service (with the possible exception of food service) because patients and visitors can observe many of its results.

MEDICAL AUDIOVISUAL SERVICE

The medical audiovisual service of a healthcare organization employs staff members who are proficient in using such audiovisual techniques as photography, sound recording, videotaping, art, exhibits, movies, and slide presentations to assist other staff members and departments in visual presentations and concepts. It is also designed to help various medical, research, and administrative staff members communicate their activities extramurally for the benefit of the medical and lay community. Its efforts are especially important at this time as the volume of medical information and technology is increasing so rapidly and the dissemination of this information is so vital.

Education and Experience

Because of the diverse and complex scientific, medical, and managerial subject matter that needs to be interpreted visually or graphically, an understanding of the relationship of the individual disciplines and their subspecialties to the specific areas of medical illustration and photography must be developed.

The medical photographer must not only be aware of the most effective photographic techniques that can be used but also must have a working knowledge of medical terminology and subject matter, which is gained only through experience. Being certified by the Biological Association as a registered biological photographer provides standards to measure individual levels of competency.

The audiovisual specialist is responsible for maintaining and operating all healthcare organization sound, videotape, and projection equipment and for recording, editing, and producing color television tapes for teaching and research purposes. The audiovisual specialist's qualifications must include a basic knowledge of sound, projection, and video equipment.

Medical illustration ideally requires a bachelor's degree in art with emphasis on medical or scientific subjects, together with thorough art training. A substitute for formal training is years of on-the-job experience under the direction of a formally trained medical illustrator.

Functions

Audiovisual services provides photography, artwork, or a combination of both through slide presentations, movies, published articles, television programs, television productions, exhibits, and displays or demonstrations.

A typical service function may occur in the following manner. If a new concept or procedure has been developed, the development must be communicated effectively to others so that they can put it to use. A graphic portrayal of the procedure is usually needed to establish reference points for developing this understanding because of the complex subject matter of medical information—a picture is, after all, worth a thousand words. Medical photographs and illustrations may become part of a written report to the medical profession, in addition to being filed in the patient's permanent medical record. Many more techniques are available for portraying various subjects and activities graphically for many purposes designed to improve medical knowledge.

Interdepartmental Relationships

Staff members of audiovisual services meet and work with members of nearly every other department in the healthcare organization, including the administrator and all of those in the medical, paramedical, and managerial professions. They also work with ancillary services and arrange for the successful staging of audiographic programs. The audiovisual staff must understand the needs of each individual or department that requests its services.

MATERIALS MANAGEMENT AND PURCHASING

The materials management and purchasing function may be described simply as buying the needed quantity and quality of an item at the proper time and the right price. The complete purchasing function, however, involves much more than buying an item. It represents a combination of responsibilities that arise from the buying transaction and other related activities. The materials management and purchasing agent not only makes the purchase but also handles the supplies in stock, engages in research, secures information to do an effective purchasing job, and assumes management responsibilities similar to those of other departments.

Complexity of Materials Management and Purchasing

Perhaps as a result of the ever-changing health services industry, numerous systems changes extend into the materials management and purchasing department where simply bargaining for the best price has been complicated by standardization, capitation, and a wide range of expense management strategies.

Although the actual buying transaction may not differ from that of other industries or of any large institution, the unique nature of the healthcare organization makes peculiar demands on materials management and purchasing. The medical goal of service to the patient makes the obligations of this function more demanding than those of other industries, whose goals are primarily to provide a product or service for profit. The overall educational level of the healthcare organization staff, increased specialization, and the staff's basic humanitarian attitude are some of the conditions that the healthcare organization's materials management and purchasing agent must consider when making decisions.

Not only are healthcare organizations increasingly specializing, but each department within an institution is involved in setting its own goals and standards of individual patient care. The materials management and purchasing agent often deals with a department as if it were an organization in itself. Because a patient's health can never be measured on any dollars-and-cents basis, materials management must incorporate into the buying process the standards of optimum healthcare that prevail within the institution and community. In a healthcare organization, it has been customary for individual department heads to set the specifications needed for their particular purchases. This presents a real challenge to the purchasing agent's diplomacy in instituting sound purchasing practices, such as standardization.

The actual number of items obtained by materials management and purchasing greatly exceeds the requirements of an average industry. The specialization and wide range of services provided make necessary a broader range of materials; unfortunately, not many items can be purchased in common for use in all or in a majority of the departments. The department must continuously apply the knowledge of specific requirement necessary to acquire each item needed.

A number of new techniques are being used for acquisition and control of inventory. These techniques depend on the type of healthcare organization, its financial conditions, cash flow, and storage capability.

One such technique is a consistent program, which is a purchasing program where supplies are ordered and shipped but not paid for until they are actually issued from inventory to a department. Another technique is a stockless program where very little or no stock is left on hand at the healthcare organization. Items are requisitioned from a major supplier as needed and are delivered directly to the ordering department. In the broadest sense, materials management in a healthcare organization encompasses the complete flow of materials from the point of a department's initial requisition up to the time of their use. This also includes items returned as rejected, not feasible to use, or in need of repair. This concept provides for the complete centralization of all materials used in the flow of goods at the healthcare organization. Centralization makes possible maximum efficiency in using personnel and materials-handling equipment and in organizing all resources to respond immediately to all departmental needs. Such a concept consolidates, under a centralized department, the sections commonly described as materials management and purchasing, receiving and storage, property and inventory control, materials handling, and the warehouse.

Centralized Materials Management and Purchasing

Materials management and purchasing in the healthcare organization has ranged from complete decentralization, in which the requesting department makes all arrangements for purchasing the item and is directly responsible to the accounting department, to the centralized control of purchasing, in which the department head originates only the specifications needed to fulfill the department's particular requirements. For many years, most healthcare organizations used the decentralized method of purchasing, relying on the department heads for leadership. This method still exists in some healthcare organizations today. The only advantage to this system is that the individual making the purchase probably is the one who knows exactly what will fit the needs of his or her department. There are, however, obvious disadvantages. Under decentralized purchasing, there can be no quantity ordering of materials that may be used in several different departments. Further, it is difficult in a decentralized system to study properly and control for the stock requirements that differ from department to department.

Centralization does not necessarily take away a department head's right to order particular equipment or supplies; it does require, however, a cooperative arrangement between the department head and the purchasing agent. Because the responsibility for all purchases in the healthcare organization lies with the purchasing agent (with appropriate administrative approval), no purchase in a centralized system should be made until the purchasing agent has been made aware of the situation and has personally signed the purchase order. In this way, the purchasing agent can then canvass the market, comparing the quantities and prices of various brands, and buy on the most economical basis.

The centralized operation greatly enhances relationships with the vendors that serve the hospital. A vendor with a question knows whom to contact and who maintains the records and information needed for smooth-running service to the healthcare organization. Vendors coming to the facility have a central reference point from which to start; thus, they do not have to waste time finding the appropriate employee. In addition, the healthcare organization will not have unauthorized people wandering around.

The concentration of the materials management and purchasing activity allows for another important advantage. The purchasing agent who researches new products, market trends, and economic indicators can supply individual department heads with complete sets of facts, relieving them of the responsibility for discovering all of this information themselves.

Stockpiling items commonly used offers advantages in control and quantity buying. Inventory review should be done periodically to update stock levels on all of the items, rather than on an ongoing basis in which receipt and issuance of items are accounted for on a form. It is this inventory control that can result on some savings for a facility that centralizes its materials management.

In any organization as specialized and as complex as many healthcare organizations, there can be arbitrary exceptions to central materials management and purchasing. Two common modifications are pharmaceutical purchasing and purchasing by the dietary department. The degree of specialization involved and the speed and urgency sometimes required in the purchase of drugs make it necessary for the pharmacy to control its own ordering. The individualized training necessary to buy food items justifies that authority be delegated to a qualified dietitian.

Functions

As a separate, well-defined position, a purchasing agent's job is one of the newer specialties found in healthcare organizations. Because of this newness and the variation of the materials management and purchasing function in different organizations, the extent of authority will vary with the administrative philosophy. The areas of responsibility commonly delegated to the purchasing agent are procuring the items, which includes appraising the needs of the institution, coordinating specifications with the person who ordered the item, selecting the vendor, arranging for the goods to be purchased, following-up on delivery, and storing and distributing the materials.

Supporting the function of procurement are record keeping, market and product research, inventory control, and management duties. Research consists of compiling and maintaining basic information on supplies and equipment that is pertinent to the buying process. The study of both product and economic market information requires the continual attention of a purchasing agent. He or she must be aware not only of what is currently on the market, but also of products pending and forthcoming.

Staff

The concept of a purchasing agent (or materials manager) as a manager arose with the advent of centralized purchasing. The agent is in a staff position, reporting directly to the administration of the healthcare organization. The administration and the agent together formulate the policies and procedures that establish the framework of the materials management and purchasing department. In addition to the previously mentioned functions, this "director of materials management" faces the task of managing the purchasing department itself and, in many cases, a combination of other support departments as well (e.g., central supply, distribution, engineering, and environmental services). The purchasing agent's increased duties and the increased expenditures made on materials by a healthcare organization have rendered the amount of paperwork and other department activities much greater than in the past.

Whether the agent has an assistant depends on the size of the purchasing department. If an organization does significant amounts of purchasing, the help of buyers is required. A buyer has a particular group of supplies or equipment for which he or she goes through the entire buying process, which may include matching the requested specifications, identifying a source or sources, requesting price information, determining appropriate source, and purchasing the item(s). A buyer logically may be delegated to purchase either medical and surgical supplies, capital equipment, or daily-use items, for example. Buyers require special knowledge of the items they are to purchase.

A standard communication device that the purchasing department uses in dealing with vendors is the purchase order. Typing purchase orders—which include the vendor's name, specifications, and other pertinent data—and taking care of the volume of paperwork necessitate the formation of clerical positions. Electronic orders are now being transmitted between healthcare organizations and major vendors, making knowledge of computerized order systems essential.

RECEIVING

Receiving the delivered materials, together with verifying that the deliveries correspond exactly with specifications on the purchase order, is commonly performed by a specifically defined section—receiving. This department may be combined with the storeroom and warehouse functions because much of the material delivered is not sent directly to departments but may be put into a central storeroom area for later distribution. Receiving and storeroom personnel are also responsible for filling requisitions for storeroom items that originate in various departments and, in many cases, for accomplishing their actual delivery. From the standpoint of the internal audit, it has been recommended that the receiving department report to an authority separate from the purchasing department. This separation provides an additional checks-and-balances system against any discrepancies in the purchasing and receiving of goods.

Interdepartmental Relationships

The purchase order form used between purchasing and a vendor is a legal contract. The handling of this form and of the initial requisition more than adequately demonstrates the interrelationships between materials management and purchasing and other departments. When the department has received a requisition detailing the specifications required by a department head for the particular purchase, these specifications are placed on the purchase order, along with other terms of the contract, such as the vendor, method of shipment, price per unit, total amount, date, and department ordering the purchase. It is a numbered form so that efficient records can be kept, and it must be signed by the authorized person, usually the purchasing agent, before it is sent to the vendor.

A purchase order is a multipart form. The original and second copy may go to the vendor or firm from which the purchase is made. By signing and returning the second copy, the vendor confirms the transaction. A third copy may go to the receiving department for notations concerning receipt of shipment. The fourth copy goes to the business office to be matched with the invoice for payment. The fifth copy stays in the purchasing department file for future reference and follow-up. Because all orders follow this logical sequence, the purchasing transaction can originate in any department of the institution and may be computerized. Purchasing, therefore, like most other staff services, involves the entire healthcare organization. It works in conjunction with receiving to coordinate incoming and outgoing shipments and with accounting to ensure prompt and accurate payment.

A Look to the Future

A healthcare organization's materials management and purchasing department will go through dramatic—and traumatic—change and will continue to grow in importance in the coming decade. Reimbursement, technology, and consumers, whether alone or together, will be the forces that will continue to shape healthcare organization materials management and purchasing. The role of "centralized" materials management and purchasing, however, may diminish in the future as it becomes more decentralized and is folded into the business areas of those who manage several service departments of the organization.

ENGINEERING AND PLANT OPERATIONS

The Joint Commission requires that healthcare organizations provide safe, functional, and effective environments for patients, staff members, and other individuals. This environment-of-care goal is supported by numerous and specific JCAHO performance standards, ranging from construction specifications to emergency drills and from equipment testing to utility systems function. Engineering and plant operations is responsible for assuring compliance with these numerous and rigid performance standards.

Specially trained professional and technical staff are needed in a healthcare organization to maintain and repair the machinery and to handle the distribution lines of the essential utility services in accordance to the environment-of-care standards set forth by the Joint Commission. This department's services are normally taken for granted, but their interruption for any length of time can cause catastrophic difficulties.

Technical and Professional Staff

Realizing the importance of these services, most healthcare organizations are now employing a graduate professional engineer or a person equally qualified in engineering and plant operations. This director of engineering and plant operations, or healthcare organization engineer, is accountable for maintaining the physical plant and its equipment. And, in the interest of administrative efficiency, this professional in some cases may be assigned the departments of laundry and environmental services. The facility engineer should also advise on any remodeling or new construction for future expansion. In addition to regular assignments, this key department director should supervise the organization's fire and safety programs.

The size and composition of the engineering and maintenance staff vary according to the extent of services the organization provides. Some facilities may negotiate a contract with outside services provided by the facility, and they may also negotiate a contract with outside services for part of their work.

Mechanical Services

The boilers and steam equipment comprise an essential portion of the institution's mechanical services. The plant operations staff must adhere to state regulations governing the use of certified stationary engineers to operate the boiler equipment. It is also a requirement that a comprehensive preventive maintenance program for the equipment and distribution lines be conducted by the engineering personnel.

The engineering staff should demonstrate expertise in refrigeration, air-conditioning, and power sources. The electrical and water supplies are also assigned to the engineering staff unless the organization employs a separate electrician and plumber.

The department plumber installs and repairs piping systems and fitting for water, steam, and drainage. The electrician is assigned the responsibilities of installing, testing, and repairing the electrical light and power distribution circuits, including those required for specialized equipment.

The rapid advancement in technology of electronic equipment has also led some healthcare organizations to establish a separate department of electronic instrumentation for the repair and development of these specialized apparatuses.

The environmental health specialist, a recent addition to healthcare organizations, creates and coordinates an effective, sustained program both for environmental health and for control of patient comfort in coordination with other departments. Specialization in environment and sanitation problems requires an educational emphasis on preventive medicine as it relates to environmental health.

Maintenance Services

Other jobs need to be done in any healthcare organization to maintain the physical appearance of the physical plant, to expand or renovate areas, and to support preventive maintenance programs. Groundskeepers, carpenters, and painters are found in most maintenance service departments.

An organization may even establish its own construction crew if the condition of the physical plant or proposed expansion indicates such a need. The ever-shifting emphasis on medical programs may make it necessary, for instance, to turn a storage area into a modern cardiac catheterization laboratory. The use of facility-based personnel in many cases could reduce the renovation costs.

Interdepartmental Relationships

Failure to meet plant department responsibilities can have a negative effect throughout the healthcare organization. Every department depends on mechanical services and at some time needs the services of maintenance personnel.

To keep complete records, the business office must have the utility (electricity, heat, water, etc.), service, and maintenance program cost reports. These figures are included to determine reimbursement on costs that the government and insurance companies use as the basis for payment of patient services.

6

Administrative Support Services

S upport services provides much-needed assistance to several key functions within healthcare organizations and can include business services, medical records, human resources, public relations,
fundraising, and marketing. Support services can be viewed using the
following "customer service" analogy: The primary customer in a healthcare
organization is the patient, and the direct caregivers—physicians, nurses,
therapists, etc.—provide health services to their primary customer—the
patient. The support staff, represented by the services mentioned above,
provide support services to internal customers—the direct caregivers. The
point of this analogy is that the health professionals (direct caregivers) would
be unable to provide quality health services without the help and assistance
provided by administrative support services. Among the administrative services introduced in this chapter are the business office, reception and information, accounting, medical records services, human resources, public
relations, fundraising, marketing, and research.

BUSINESS SERVICES

Business services is responsible for ensuring that proper procedures are in
place to manage the organization's admitting and registration functions
efficiently, to record in a timely manner the charges to the patient's account
and third-party billing requirements, and to collect all funds due the organization. The responsibility for overseeing other departments typically falls

under the direction of the director of business services. Within this section, the common reporting departments are admitting and all registration areas, patient accounting, patient and insurance billing, and cashiering.

Director of Financial Services

The administrative head of business services may be called the chief financial officer (CFO), controller, director of finance, or business services director. The title usually implies responsibility for acting as an adviser to the administrator and board of directors on financial policy, and for long-range financial planning. The controller sets procedures for all accounting duties performed in the institution whether the personnel involved in this work report directly to him or her. As CFO, reporting to the administrator, this manager is responsible for receiving and depositing all money that is received, whatever its source. The head of business services also approves the payment of salaries and other expenditures and maintains detailed records of all incoming and outgoing transactions of funds. The position therefore requires at least basic skills in accounting. One of the accountant's most important tools is a system of cost accounting that shows the allocation of cost to each program. All of this helps to assure members of the public that they are receiving the maximum in health services for every dollar spent. The discipline of "cost accounting" strengthens the position of the healthcare organization when negotiating managed care contracts. Cost accounting provides the health service provider with information needed to determine the actual cost of providing different types and levels of patient care.

The controller should have a bachelor's degree, usually in accounting or business administration. Postcollege business experience should include some years of responsible accounting work, with supervisory responsibilities, in an accredited healthcare organization.

A Look to the Future

Integrated business services continues to grow in significance wherein business office staff members are trained in both billing and collections and are specialized according to payors. The advantages of a payor-specific process is more efficient contact with major payor groups and better-trained, more-flexible staff.

With the introduction of prospective payment in the health services industry, the healthcare organizations accounts' role will continue to change from reimbursement maximizer to important roles in decision making. Faced with increased competition, healthcare organizations will continue to install a variety of financial controls.

ADMITTING SERVICES

The patient usually makes his or her first contact with a healthcare organization during admitting. The efficiency and sensitivity of the admitting personnel greatly influence not only the patient but also the relatives and friends who accompany the patient. The combination of competent, diplomatic personnel and good admission procedures can do much to relieve the underlying emotions that intensify the trauma of an illness.

Staff

The healthcare organization's admitting department is under the direction of an admitting manager. Sometimes the admitting manager is a professional nurse, but in recent years, more people with degrees in specialties ranging from psychology to business administration have entered this field. A general knowledge of the institution's policies and of the community's social and economic conditions should be a prerequisite for holding this position. Large admitting departments have an assistant admitting manager to share the responsibility. Personnel in the department must possess clerical skills.

Department Organization

In larger healthcare organizations, admitting staff may report to the director of business services or may be part of a separate department, reporting directly to administration. In smaller institutions an admitting officer may handle the admitting department and perform other duties as well. Although the structures mentioned previously are the most common, the admission and discharge function is so tightly integrated with so many departments that a universally accepted line of administrative reporting cannot be precisely drawn.

Patient Admission

A patient can be admitted only after consulting with a physician who has recommended admission to a hospital or other healthcare organization. At the time of a person's admission as an inpatient or outpatient, medical and sociological data that will be used for reference by different healthcare team personnel are obtained. This information will be used not only for medical purposes but also for credit arrangements for the patient's stay, health insurance information, consent forms, numerous other incidental data, and a specific bed or clinic assignment. Utilization and concurrent review continues to be a dominant practice, which means that the physician or any other provider of healthcare services must contact the third-party payor and

obtain authorization before having the patient admitted. Admitting personnel verify this authorization.

Collecting this information at a central point—the admitting office—
requires a substantial amount of clerical support because the patient's admission information has to be cataloged and routed to the proper departments. This task is accomplished by using an admission packet containing
specially designed forms that are filled out with information from the patient or relative at the time of admission. To make the patient's admission as
smooth and efficient as possible, some facilities have tried various methods
to obtain certain information before admission. Electronic data processing
is making obsolete many of the clerical tasks in the admitting office. The
information goes directly into a computer to be dispersed where it is needed.

At the time of admission, the patient has usually been assigned by his or
her physician to a schedule of laboratory tests, usually routine, and to an
admission diet so that a specific meal will be prepared for the patient during
the next meal period.

Patient Discharge

It logically follows that the discharge of an inpatient is accomplished by the
admitting department. The patient may be discharged home or to another
healthcare organization, but the procedure is basically the same.

Patients are usually discharged only on the order of their attending physician, although a patient may leave at will at any time unless he or she has
been legally committed. When the admitting department has been notified
of the pending discharge, the credit arrangements should be satisfied, documentation of the medical aspects of the stay must be complete and in order,
and all of the departments involved with the patient need to be informed of
the discharge. Coordination of all of these activities at discharge helps eliminate late charges against the patient's bill, which are more difficult to collect once the patient has been discharged.

Inpatient Census

As an adjunct to the process of checking admissions, discharges, and deaths,
the admissions department usually prepares the daily census report, which
is based on information supplied by each patient area of the healthcare organization. The patient unit informs the admitting department of the total
number of patients and of the transfer of any patient to another bed. For the
maximum utilization of beds, the admitting department must know the
location of each patient's bed assignment.

At times, a healthcare organization may have a high occupancy rate. By
knowing the exact patient occupancy count and bed assignments—and

by using an advance reservation record—the admitting department can efficiently achieve a uniform level of patient occupancy.

The precise scheduling of patients requires that services other than a bed also be available when a particular patient is admitted. For example, the operating room schedule is coordinated with the admitting department to ensure that patients requiring surgery will have operating room services accessible to them.

Interdepartmental Relationships

The admission procedure begins with the patient's physician who requests the admitting department to admit the patient. Paramedical departments such as nursing, dietary, environmental services, and laboratory must be aware of the impending admission and must make the necessary preparations. Environmental services and nursing coordinate their duties of cleaning a discharged patient's room to prepare it for the scheduled admission. There should be no loss in revenue to the healthcare organization or inconvenient delay to the admitted patient if the cleaning has been accomplished. When a patient is discharged, similar information flow is used to prevent the dietary department from preparing an unnecessary meal or the pharmacy from preparing inpatient medications.

The emergency room has presented a unique problem for the admitting department. Obtaining information from an emergency patient is a delicate task. The records taken in an emergency room should receive special consideration and should be as complete as possible. Some facilities have admitting personnel stationed in the emergency departments.

INFORMATION AND RECEPTION SERVICES

The release of information about a patient involves many moral and legal considerations that must be taken into account. Most organizations have established a central source for release of patient information. The need for this central source, as well as the necessity of providing assistance to visitors and other persons entering the building, have led many healthcare organizations to construct a reception area near the main entrance. This area is staffed by personnel familiar with both the organization's physical layout and with the procedures regarding visitors, sales representatives, and patients. Under the proper guidance, volunteers provide an excellent source of staffing for this area.

Inquiries about the condition of a patient are usually directed to the reception. The nursing units release specific information about a patient with care taken to inform a friend or relative satisfactorily without infringing on the patient's right of confidentiality. No information should be released contrary to the express wishes of the patient. Many healthcare organizations have a consent form for the release of information that is signed by the patient at the time of admission.

Newspaper personnel and other media representatives often ask to be provided with information. On a limited basis, the information and reception area can provide some facts. For more specific information or in the event of a disaster, public relations should be the source for release of facts.

A Look to the Future

Automation of patient admissions and discharge procedures continues to evolve in today's healthcare organizations. Technological advances in these important services have resulted in significant and much-needed benefits. With increasing pressures on healthcare organizations to reduce operating expenses, enhanced automation of the patient admissions and discharge process will continue to evolve. The importance of preadmission programs will continue to increase in light of the trend toward shorter lengths of stay. New processes are required to prepare patients for same-day admission, to initiate discharge planning at the earliest possible opportunity, and to provide education to patients for which there is now less time during hospitalization.

ACCOUNTING

Accounting is the center of operation for all of the healthcare organization's financial affairs. The rising costs of providing patient care, combined with reduced reimbursement, have placed added emphasis on the soundness of an organization's fiscal condition. Proper accounting methods are of great value in the orderly recording of income and expenditures and in providing statistics for organizational analysis.

Staff

As one of the key staff members in accounting, the accountant prepares periodic financial and statistical reports, including those on cash receipts, accounts receivable, payroll, and other expenses. The minimum requirements for such a position are college-level accounting courses or equivalent on-the-job training.

Other positions in the accounting department include personnel with bookkeeping knowledge and experience. The number of staff assigned to the department is related to the organization's size and the scope of its activities. Special skills in electronic data processing have become necessary in most accounting departments.

Payroll

With payroll costs amounting to nearly half of its operating expenditures, the healthcare organization must be prepared to present the employee with an accurate paycheck and to provide adequate accounting for bookkeeping and analysis.

The basis for preparing a payroll check is time reporting, and a variety of methods can be used as a source of record for payroll. The time card, either filled out by hand or automatically by insertion in a time clock, is much like the standard one used in other industries. Daily time sheets verified by a supervisor furnish another suitable reporting vehicle.

Once the payroll information has been reported, the payroll check is calculated and written. At the same time, federal withholding tax, social security, and other deductions are recorded on the employee's record and the institution's payroll register. The figures accumulated in the payroll register are then included as expenditures in the budgets of the applicable departments.

General Ledger

The cornerstone of any accounting system is the general ledger, which summarizes all financial transactions by showing the total information that is recorded in detail elsewhere. For example, the amount patients owed is recorded in detail in the patient accounts receivable subsidiary ledger, but the total amount due is shown in the general ledger.

Cost-based Reimbursement

Substantial differences in rates that institutions were charging the government for similar services gave rise to the need for a comparatively equitable method of reimbursement. Under the principle of cost-based reimbursement, government agencies and commercial insurance companies pay the healthcare organization the costs of providing the service. Tracking and proper reporting of costs under this method of reimbursement are critical to the institution's financial health.

In recent years, the use of cost-based reimbursement by the Medicare program has diminished significantly. Beginning on October 1, 1983, the Medicare program started to reimburse inpatient acute care services under the prospective payment system. This method of reimbursement established a flat payment amount depending on the type of illness treated. Illness types are categorized into approximately 470 DRGs, each with its own reimbursement amount based on the location of the provider and the intensity of the services required. Only under certain specific circumstances, such as an unusually long stay, may the provider receive reimbursement beyond the designated DRG amount. Cost-based reimbursement continues to be used by the Medicare program to pay for the majority of outpatient services performed by an acute care facility and for all services rendered in an SNF.

In addition to monitoring reimbursement (cost-based and prospective payment), cost reporting can provide a good analysis and summary of the organization's operations.

Capital and Operating Budgets

A budget is a formal presentation of expenses and revenues—as well as of the capital requirements (building and equipment)—that are expected at a future time, usually during the fiscal year. In preparing a budget, management carefully correlates its expectations of the demand for personnel and supplies in all departments with the anticipated revenue for the same period. These forecasts, translated into dollar values, are presented in report form for each department and for the healthcare organization as a whole. Collectible charges to patients should then be reviewed and adjusted to meet the cost of operation, including capital requirements.

CREDIT AND COLLECTION

Although government and private insurance companies pay a large part of our country's total net revenue for healthcare, individuals still pay a substantial amount of the nation's healthcare budget. The ability to collect its share is significant to the organization despite the increase in other reimbursements. Because of the episodic nature of illness, a healthcare organization can find itself forced either to grant more credit than any other single business or to refuse service to the patient.

The responsibility to collect the balance incurred by patients lies with the business office. Under the direction of a business office manager, the department advises patients on the healthcare organization's policy concerning credit, examines the patients on their particular financial situation, and helps establish equitable payment plans.

The Patient's Account

Commencing with the admission interview, the patient's account requires continual follow-up to prevent delinquency of payment. Information from the interview is compiled as a basis for establishing a credit rating. Upon assessing the patient's ability to afford the financial burden of illness, the interviewer recommends an appropriate payment procedure to ensure the best chance of collection that is most consistent with the patient's financial status.

If the institution is unable to collect the balance of the account when the patient is discharged, alternative credit arrangements are made. The patient then receives an updated statement, usually monthly, showing his or her balance. Should this account show delinquency of payment, a series of collection letters of increasing urgency is sent to the patient. Telephone calls may also be used in combination with the collection letters. If payments cannot be collected, the credit manager may turn the account over to a collection agency, an action that should be taken only if the other methods have not succeeded because the collection agency receives a substantial fee for its services.

The final disposition of an inactive patient account is to consider it uncollectible. The credit manager, with the approval of the controller, usually writes off an uncollectible account after six months.

A competent business office should temper its persistence with the knowledge of the effect of the burden of illness on the patient.

MEDICAL RECORD SERVICES

Although the subject of information management is discussed in a subsequent chapter, it is acknowledged that the medical record services of healthcare organizations are at the very core of information management. Fundamentally, this information has to do with patient medical information and reimbursement for health services rendered. Recently, medical records has become regarded as a revenue department in that the accuracy and completeness of the medical record relates directly to fiscal reimbursement to the healthcare provider.

For each patient who receives medical care, a complete and accurate statement of medical facts must be compiled and retained. This statement is a permanent document giving the history and progress of one person's illness or injury; it represents all of the observations and findings recorded by the patient's physician and other members of the organization's paramedical staff.

The Joint Commission acknowledges that healthcare delivery to patients is a complex process that depends highly on information. Healthcare organizations rely on information about the science of care, individual patients, care provided and results of care, as well as its ability to provide, coordinate, and integrate services. Medical records has primary responsibility for these information management initiatives.

The Joint Commission further states that medical records are important tools in the practice of medicine. They serve as a basis for planning patient care and provide a means of communication between the physician and other professional groups contributing to the patient's care. Such records furnish documentary evidence of the course of the patient's illness and treatment, and they serve as a basis for review, study, and evaluation of the medical care rendered to the patient. For these reasons, the Joint Commission considers the quality of medical records an important indication of the quality of patient care given in a hospital.

Staff

Establishing and maintaining a medical record system that is accurate and accessible is the responsibility of the record administrator and staff. The medical record administrator's professional education usually consists of a four-year undergraduate program in medical records science from an approved school. Approved schools are those with four-year programs in accredited colleges and universities that grant a bachelor's degree in medical records administration or medical records science, or those that also give postgraduate work in medical records science. Upon completion of the approved professional program, the graduate is eligible to take the registration examination, given by the American Medical Record Association (AMRA), to achieve the title of registered record administrator.

Through their work with the medical staff, medical record administrators are usually invited to become members of the organization's utilization review committee; the quality assurance committee, which reviews patient's charts, conducts audits, and maintains statistics to determine the quality of medical care; and the medical records committee. In some organizations, these duties may all be combined under one committee structure. It is important that the department also have its views represented concerning the design of the forms used in the medical record.

Medical record technician

Assisting the medical record administrator in the technical work of maintaining medical records, reports, disease indexes, and healthcare statistics is the medical record technician. This position is a result of the increased demand placed on the medical record department for accurate and accessible record keeping. Schools for medical record technicians are approved by the AMA's Council on Medical Education. Only graduates of approved schools for medical record technicians or those who complete the AMRA's correspondence course may qualify to take the examination to become an accredited record technician. Then, they can assist the physician in preparing reports, transcribing histories of patients and reports of their physical examinations, and checking the patient's records to ensure that all information is complete and accurate, according to prescribed standards, and coded according to an accepted diagnostic nomenclature.

Also assisting medical records are the clerical staff, who organize charts, code diseases for DRGs and other purposes, maintain the files, transcribe dictation, and handle other routine department business.

Functions

According to Joint Commission standards, the functions of medical records may be divided under two broad headings: administrative and medical. The following item from Hospital Accreditation References describes the administrative and medical activities of most medical record departments (JCAHO 1997).

Administrative functions

These functions include:

1. maintaining a medical record on all patients admitted for care in a hospital;
2. preserving these records for a period of time as determined by law and hospital policies;
3. maintaining a system of identification and filing to ensure location of patients' records;
4. centralizing all clinical information pertaining to patients' records; and
5. indexing records according to disease, operation, and physician.

Medical functions

These functions include ensuring that:

1. the medical records contain sufficient medical and clinical information;
2. only authorized personnel obtain information from the various sections of the medical records; and
3. records are signed and authenticated by authorized personnel.

Although these activities are the primary functions of medical records, broader implications exist. Because different uses for the patient record have developed, medical records has had to expand its functions from the original concept of record keeping. The patient record has become a source of statistics for administration, for physicians undertaking research, and for staff engaged in educational programs. It contains information of legal value and is referred to by attorneys, the courts, and insurance companies. Most recently, the government requirement for patient care evaluation and peer review has created great activity in the review of medical records. Government agencies reason that the medical record is the only documented evidence of the quality of the care given a patient. Agencies at all governmental levels, and a variety of healthcare programs, also require statistical information from these records, further increasing the demands made on the department.

Compiling these statistics can consist of noting the number of patients admitted or discharged for service on each day, totaling these statistics by day, month, and year.

Medical records is also responsible for completing diagnostic coding information for insurance forms. With Medicare and private insurance companies paying a large portion of the patient's bills, it has become of utmost importance that this vital service be performed accurately and on a timely basis. Accuracy in coding is now tied directly into proper reimbursement and has never been more important than in today's managed care environment.

In most healthcare organizations, transcribing doctors' notes, histories, physical examinations, and various other material generated by the physician in the course of treatment is handled by medical records.

Filing Systems

Because medical records is, in effect, a library of patient information files, a prime consideration in its effective functioning is the positioning of storage and retrieval areas. Filing systems are obviously important because a medical record is of no use if it cannot be retrieved. In the unit-numbering system, the patient receives a number on his or her first admission as an inpatient or outpatient and retains that number on all subsequent admissions to any department. Under this system, all admissions are filed together in one folder and under one number.

Other important considerations in medical records' physical layout are the space involved, the types of shelving used in the file room, the dictating equipment for the physician's use, and the design of the chart (medical record) folder.

Tumor Registry

Other statistics kept by medical records are particular disease indexes. The most frequently kept is the tumor registry, which usually consists of three parts. The first part is an abstract of the patient's chart, which gives the pertinent details about the disease. The second part is the follow-up procedure, in which the patient is followed through life so that valuable data for both epidemiologic research and clinical research can be accumulated. Medical records is usually responsible for continuing this follow-up. The third part of the tumor registry is the reporting. Although yearly reports on the data are required for various accreditation agencies, the most valuable use of these data can be made by those clinicians and researchers who are either treating a similar malignancy or conducting research on treatment and causes.

Classification of Disease

To classify diseases into a form that is easily identifiable, medical records uses the ICD-9-CM coding scheme. These codes essentially assign a number to a disease or surgical procedure. The department codes all diseases and operations by those numbers and can then easily locate a particular disease category through a group of charts of patients having that particular disease.

The Medical Record

The actual medical record chart comprises many components. The first part consists of a face sheet or admitting sheet, which should contain all identifying information of a sociological/demographic nature, as well as all data necessary for indexing the particular case. It provides space for signatures of attending physicians (such signatures are required by many agencies). It usually contains the provisional or working diagnosis, which is only an opinion given at or near the time of admission, based on the physician's incomplete knowledge about the case. The final diagnoses, which should be recorded upon the patient's discharge, is the statement of the attending physician, complete and accurate after extensive study.

The next item in the chart is the history section, which contains pertinent information regarding present illness, past history, family and social history, and a complete physical examination done by the physician in the admitting department. The laboratory portion of the chart should contain all laboratory findings; one of medical records' duties is to audit the doctor's order sheet to ensure that all test results are indeed recorded. All other diagnostic aids, such as x-ray films and electrocardiograms, are also checked against the physician's order sheet for completion.

The progress notes usually come next, and these should be specific statements written by the attending physician regarding the disease's course. They represent the physician's observations and complement those noted in the nurse's bedside record. The medical record department should ensure that these observations are present and signed by the physician recording them. A discharge summary must be included in the medical record and should be a concise record of the essential information regarding the patient's illness, including the investigation, diagnosis, treatment, and future plans.

The physician's order sheet, which is a record of all orders given by the physician, is checked to be sure that they are all signed by the attending physician (or by the intern or resident with the attending physician's approval). The nursing notes, which are a bedside record of the patient's progress observed by the nursing staff on the unit, should be present and should be checked for continuity and the necessary signatures. Most charts also contain a section of graphs where the patient's temperature, pulse, and respiration should be recorded.

The medical record must contain many special reports. If surgery is performed, there must be an operative report as well as an anesthesiologist's report. If a specimen was sent for examination by a pathologist, a pathology report must be present. If there was a consultation, this too should be part of the medical record. Other types of special reports are the transfusion record, recovery room record, autopsy report (if required), and some less commonly used special forms such as a diabetic record. The medical record must also contain special authorization documents, such as consent to treat, consent to operate, or consent to perform an autopsy.

Interdepartmental Relationships

Because the medical record is a cumulative document of the patient's stay in the healthcare organization or of outpatient treatment, medical records is necessarily related to all departments that produce patient information. This relationship starts with the patient's admission process. The face sheet and physical examination forms, which represent the first information to appear in the patient's medical record, may be initiated in the admitting department. During the patient's stay, all departments involved in his or her care are transmitting information; the clerical staff place these data in the medical record.

Employees in many departments require information contained in the medical record. It may serve, for example, as a source of information to the business office for charging and billing for patient services. It becomes a source of statistical data for medical and paramedical research and of data that can help the administration organize services more efficiently. The pharmacist may check it for medication orders, dosage, time and method of administering a drug, and discontinuation of the drug. The nurse constantly refers to the chart to check the physician's orders and the patient's test results, as well as to enter observations. Other paramedical personnel, such as physical therapists, occupational therapists, and social workers, refer to the chart and enter progress notes. Recording all activity centering on the patient makes the medical record a necessary and useful document of the patient's medical care.

HUMAN RESOURCE SERVICES IN HEALTHCARE ORGANIZATIONS

Because approximately 65 percent of the healthcare organization's operating expenses are represented by payroll, human resources is receiving more attention than ever from management. As many as 300 different jobs may be staffed in a large healthcare organization, a fact that indicates the complex importance of this department's functions.

Organization and Scope

Human resources' organizational position is usually one of a staff relationship to other departments, and the human resources director reports to the organization's administrator. The department's role is to develop a framework that assists the heads of the various other departments in their line responsibilities with their personnel. Applying experience and resources, human resources assists with and consults on managing and maximizing the utilization of staff. Human resources has the responsibility to develop some specific programs within this broad scope.

Functions

The organization's wage and salary program, for example, should be designed to help make employment a satisfying experience. The policies should be as fair as possible to help eliminate inequities.

Wage and salary administration

The approach to a wage and salary program is similar in most institutions. First, each job within the facility is completely evaluated, and the core of such evaluation is the job analysis.

Job analysis and job description. Job analysis is a phase in which the employee should actively participate. Pertinent information about the job's specific nature is gathered and becomes the basis for the analysis. The differences between one job and another, together with the skills and responsibilities necessary to succeed, make up the required information. When documented in a formalized statement, this information becomes the job description.

Although the job description is helpful to human resources in selecting a candidate for a job, its purpose covers a much broader range. It gives management a particular position's parameters and forms the basis for evaluating the employee's performance.

Job specifications. To help human resources determine exactly which candidate will best fit a particular job, that position's specifications are compiled and documented. These specifications include the details from the job description but may also include facts that are not directly part of the job but that will influence the selection of a particular candidate (specific time requirements for each function, for example, as well as detailed physical and special demands).

Compensation. Once human resources has the relevant data on each job, it uses a systematic method to determine the relative position of each job on the wage and salary scale. A common method is to establish a point scale for the different job factors, that is, skills and education required, the level of responsibility, and working conditions. The higher the total point score of each job, the higher the position on the salary scale.

Aided by the information on the organization's individual jobs, human resources uses community salary surveys, federal and state wage and hours laws, current labor market standards, and the cost of living as some of the guidelines to establish a minimum and maximum wage level for each job classification.

Compiling and constant updating of the organization's total wage and salary program is an ongoing process to be reported annually—along with the other portions of proposed future expenditures—to the administration and the board of directors. After the board of directors has approved the program, each employee's wage level should be adjusted according to the previously mentioned criteria. Evaluating each employee's performance provides a continuing means of equating individual job performance with monetary compensation.

Employment Program

The employment program in human resources is designed to secure the best applicants and then to select from that group the best person. Although the employment process is centralized in the human resources office, applicants are only initially screened there. The final judgment should be made by the department that requested an applicant for a position.

The hiring procedure has several stages, all of which may be used for the specific purpose of screening. The procedure usually proceeds from completion of an application form through preliminary interviews and employment tests in human resources, to verification of reference checks, a passed physical examination, and final selection by the supervisor. Depending on the situation, some stages may be added or omitted. Smaller organizations with only a small human resources department may eliminate all but its clerical function in the hiring process. Information about the job's requirements must relate closely and positively to the information about the applicant when a selection for employment is made. Because of certain employment laws, offers of employment are conditional upon the job candidates passing a pre-employment health examination and drug screen, as well as confirmation that they are legal to work within the United States.

Orientation and Training Programs

Orientation programs are designed to help the employee adjust to a new work environment. Each department may have its own formal or informal orientation, although the institution as a whole most likely has a program for new employees—usually administered by human resources. The program's objectives are to inform the new employees about the conditions of their employment and areas of education (e.g., safety and infection control) required under Joint Commission guidelines and state laws and to acquaint them with their new surroundings. The program should be supplemented with an employee handbook, which explains basic personnel policies, fringe benefits, and other pertinent information.

Besides providing the orientation program, a healthcare organization may offer job training and continuing education for employees, development of management skills for supervisory personnel, and education sessions for executive development. The degree to which human resources coordinates these programs will vary from institution to institution, from merely providing a clerical function to presenting the program completely.

As an adjunct to the on-site training programs, human resources may administer career development counseling, tuition reimbursement programs, work-study plans, organization-sponsored off-hour courses, and other continuing educational activities. Some state and national licensing boards are requiring continuing education for professional and vocational recertification, making the organization-sponsored programs an excellent benefit for both the institution and the employee.

Policies and Procedures

One important responsibility of human resources is to develop written employee policies and procedures. These are approved by administration, who in turn must receive approval for major policies from the board of directors. These policies include such items as promotion, transfer, payroll, recruitment, hiring, employee relations, and counseling. Publishing these policies and procedures in written form tends to provide consistency in the management/employee relationship. Because of the impact of such policies, it is vital for human resources to obtain information from many sources, including employees themselves.

While human resources may also participate in developing fire, disaster, and safety plans, as well as employee activities and community relations programs, its role is limited by its size and resources.

Staff

Besides the necessary clerical employees and the human resources director, the staff may include an employment recruiter, who interviews and screens job applicants. This person works with department managers and supervisors to determine the qualifications an applicant needs. The employment recruiter then uses various resources such as communications media, employment agencies, and word-of-mouth to find suitable applicants.

Equal Employment Opportunity– Affirmative Action Program

To ensure that equal opportunity does exist, equal employment opportunity has become law. Major federal laws and executive orders delineate the legal requirements that organizations must meet to ensure that employees are protected from

- employment discrimination;
- harassment in the workplace; and
- unsafe working conditions.

The federal and state statutes set forth to establish employee rights in the workplace include but are not limited to:

- Title VII of the Civil Rights Act of 1964;
- Equal Pay Act of 1963;
- Age Discrimination in Employment Act of 1990;
- Americans With Disabilities Act of 1990;
- Rehabilitation Act of 1973;
- Pregnancy Discrimination Act of 1978;
- Vietnam Veteran's Readjustment Assistance Act of 1974; and
- Immigration Reform and Control Act of 1986.

This legislation has been upheld in definitive court decisions. Thus, equal employment opportunity has had an increasingly strong effect on the way in which healthcare employers manage human resources. The legislation listed prohibits discrimination based on race, color, marital status, religion, gender, national origin, age, or a qualified physical or mental handicap in all employment practices including—but not limited to—employment, promotion, demotion or transfer; recruitment or recruitment advertising; layoff or termination; rates of pay or other forms of compensation; selection for training, including apprenticeship; benefits; and other terms and conditions of employment. Executive Order 11246 and the Rehabilitation Act of 1973 require the implementation of written affirmative action plans.

The term *equal opportunity–affirmative action* is neither redundant nor repetitious. Equal opportunity is a condition, and affirmative action is the means by which that condition is achieved. Therefore, if equality does exist, there is no need to take affirmative action.

Management involvement is the basis of an effective affirmative action program and begins with a strong company policy and written commitment. To ensure the success of the program, management must assign the responsibility and authority to implement the program to an individual in top management who has the ability to accomplish program goals.

Other essential elements of the program are overseeing external and internal dissemination of the policy; analyzing minority, female, and handicap employment by department and job classification; developing measurable and reasonable goals; establishing internal audit and reporting systems that monitor all aspects of the program; and developing training programs and services such as counseling, day care, housing, and job-related education that will assist in recruiting and retaining minorities, women, and handicapped individuals.

An effective affirmative action program is an essential aspect of good human resources management in that it assists in using the human resources and skills of minority, female, and handicapped individuals that heretofore have been underused.

A Look to the Future

Continued cost-containment initiatives, strategic organizational changes in the form of mergers and acquisitions, and various forms of affiliations between healthcare organizations will place increasing importance on—and challenge—human resources. These external and internal organizational changes resulting in variations in business volume will require flexible staffing patterns to contain costs. Additionally, it will be necessary for human resource professionals to initiate measures that result in a broader utilization of the existing work force, and this will require staff education and cross-training. A continuous search for improvement in productivity and service quality will need to be human resources' main strategic initiative within the managed care environment—an environment that continues to restrict levels of financial reimbursement to healthcare providers. As such, human resources, which oversees the largest part of the operating budget, must seek innovative ways to maximize staff utilization at the lowest possible cost.

PUBLIC RELATIONS

Public relations or communications is charged with establishing and managing an organizational communications function for the organization and its services and programs. It does so by providing support to management and by building relationships through planned communications with its various audiences. In its largest sense, it is the interpreter of the organization to its various publics. The job function typically includes both internal and external communications.

The general goal is to influence the public to support the organization's goals and objectives, which is accomplished by managing its discourse with the public and by controlling where possible how the issues facing the organization are perceived. To gain a better understanding of the multiple ways in which these tasks are carried out requires, first, listing some of the organization's typical audiences:

- former and current patients;
- patients' families and other interested parties;
- employees and their families;
- potential employees;
- physicians and potential physicians;
- third-party payors;
- legislators and government officials;
- trustees and volunteers;
- vendors;
- community representatives;
- special audiences, such as senior citizens; and
- media representatives.

The role of public relations, or communications, spans the reach of the organization, as evidenced by the list of its audiences. Public relations practitioners, then, must address the communication requirements of all the organization's staff to the various audiences and provide counseling, materials, and support. The following functions typically are carried out:

- editing and producing organizational periodicals, such as newsletters;
- managing the advertising function in support of marketing functions;

- developing corporate identity systems;
- managing press relations;
- directing crisis communications;
- providing and acting as organizational spokespersons; and
- assisting in areas closely related, such as employee relations, customer service, board relations, and community relations.

Changing Focus

In past years, the public relations function was interpreted to be a health services publicist or special events producer. That orientation has been strongly influenced by the importance of marketing the healthcare organization. In addition, a broader approach has been taken by more executives who view public relations as a direct tool and aid to management. Today, the public relations practitioner has a greater focus and concern with such issues than with merely putting healthcare organization in a good light (although that too is undertaken). The marketing orientation has benefited public relations practitioners in that they are taking more responsibility for planning and being accountable for their performance. They are also crossing the bridge from doing "nice" things to directly affecting the organization's bottom line.

Organizing the Public Relations Function

Job titles vary and reporting structures differ. A public relations manager can be a member of senior management, emphasizing the counseling aspect, or the role, can be viewed more as one of a technician handling more prescribed duties. The organization's emphasis should help determine the qualifications sought in a public relations manager. The role has strong relationships with and even overlaps duties with other functions in the organization, such as marketing, community relations, and human resources. All staff are a part of the internal communications function, and they can influence those outside of the organization. Because of this, it is important to define the precise means of operating with these areas so that all work toward a common goal.

Operations

Public relations and communications staff must assess the needs of operations departments to provide communications support. This means that the managers in operations departments are also "customers" of the public relations function, and it is important that they know the resources available to them.

It is equally important that the public relations staff assess the needs of all other audiences the organization serves and that they communicate their capabilities to those audiences. Communication planning—through media or advertising—must not only be compatible with the organization's goals but must also directly support those goals. The process generally follows these steps:

1. Identify the relevant public/stakeholders to whom communications must be directed. It is less important today to use mass communications. The more targeted the public, the better the communication and the better the results.

2. Gather information through interviews, research, audits, and surveys on the audiences and their perceptions of important issues, services, and practices.

3. Develop strategies for communicating based on that research. Test the strategies, if possible, with small groups.

4. Implement an action plan based on the strategies most likely to be effective.

5. Evaluate results and progress and share this information with the organization's management team, not only as part of a process for being accountable but also as a means of educating the staff on the importance, relevance, and impact of the communications function.

FUNDRAISING

The very foundation of the American healthcare organization is rooted in the process of fundraising or, more correctly, in philanthropy. In 1731, Benjamin Franklin appealed to the citizens of Philadelphia to fund the first hospital in New York. Since then, billions of dollars have been given to support nonprofit healthcare organizations throughout the United States. In fact, without the use of fundraising, many of this country's hospitals and other healthcare organizations simply would not exist.

Various methods and techniques are used by modern professional development officers to raise the dollars needed to meet current as well as capital needs of healthcare organizations. These methods break down into three basic groups of programs:

1. annual programs
2. capital campaigns
3. deferred or planned gift programs

Annual Programs

Annual programs are those activities defined as having a direct and immediate dollar response to their use, usually accomplished by direct mail, or direct-response programming. A letter or brochure is mailed, and a response is received within a few days or weeks. This kind of program is usually designed to acquire new donors or to upgrade present donors to a higher level of support. Special events, while considered as annual fundraising activities, usually are designed to recognize a donor or donors or to cultivate a new group of supporters. Although some healthcare organizations are very successful in having their special events raise a significant amount of money, most are designed to net, at the most, half of the gross revenue received.

Capital Campaigns

Capital campaigns or programs are designed to raise funds, usually over three to five years. A campaign can be a very effective tool for raising the funds to build new facilities, remodel present facilities, or purchase major pieces of equipment. Many institutions will retain a capital campaigns consultant to assist with these kinds of programs. More hospitals and related healthcare organizations are using the campaign format today to raise endowment funds in addition to annual revenues.

Deferred or Planned Gift Programs

Planned or deferred gifts are a critical part of any development program. These gifts are usually made in such a way that the donor gives the asset to the healthcare organization irrevocably but retains the rights to the earnings of that asset until death. It is possible to include other beneficiaries in these agreements as well so that a husband could name himself as beneficiary until his death, or vice versa, and then have the wife become the beneficiary until her death, or vice versa, with the asset and earnings going to the charity for its use only at the death of the second person. These agreements are usually called irrevocable charitable trusts. A commitment within a will to leave a specific amount to a charitable cause is also considered a deferred gift.

Many variations of these gift techniques exist, and most nonprofit healthcare organizations today have a professional funds development officer to manage and develop these programs regularly.

Over the years, philanthropy's place in the economic structure of hospitals and healthcare organizations has contracted or expanded in line with outside economic conditions—either locally or nationally. There was a time, before widespread subscription to health insurance, when philanthropy provided half of the nonprofit hospitals' capital needs. As payment for services from third-party payors became more consistent and reliable, the need to ask for and receive the community's charitable dollars declined and nearly disappeared. Today, however, government and private payors are neither able nor willing to fund every healthcare organization's total operating and expansion needs. Organizations without endowments and reserves are essentially forced into greater debt to meet shortfalls or expansion needs, or they must seek and obtain a greater flow of charitable gifts. Most will have to do both.

The capital most hospitals need today is so great that philanthropy will never be able to provide more than a relatively small portion. In view of a declining revenue base, however, philanthropy can likely provide that necessary margin to enable a healthcare organization to provide quality healthcare to its community.

Unlike the seemingly uncontrollable realities of shrinking federal and state budgets for healthcare and the erosion of private insurance offerings, the development of philanthropic support from the local community is completely within the control and discretion of the organization's board of directors and administration. The first steps toward establishing a successful philanthropic program simply require strong organizational commitment to create a systematic program that will show the community that the healthcare organization—its staff, programs, and policies—is worthy of its charitable support.

MARKETING

For the healthcare organization to flourish, closely watching the changes in the healthcare environment as well as the needs and demands of those it serves is critical. The healthcare organization must match its resources with the desires of its consumers (i.e., patients, physicians, community). Managing this dynamic relationship is the marketing's responsibility. As a formally organized department, marketing is relatively new to most healthcare organizations: Only since the early 1980s that marketing has been a widely accepted function. Today, it is regarded as a critical link between the healthcare organization's present and future.

Staff

Coordinating the healthcare organization's marketing activities requires a comprehensive understanding of the interrelationships within the delivery system as well as the ability to apply marketing concepts to healthcare. Most organizations will seek an individual who has obtained a master's degree in either healthcare administration or business administration.

The staff employed within marketing will vary depending on organization's specific needs. Because of the importance of physician relations, many marketing departments will include an individual who is responsible for communicating with physicians and other healthcare professionals on behalf of the organization. Depending on the organization's size, some marketing departments are organized according to the major products or services the organization provides. Individuals in charge of the marketing for each of these groups are similar in function to the group product manager of other consumer industries.

Activities

Through a variety of activities, marketing must translate the needs and wants of the outside environment into programs and services that best fit the organization's abilities, resources, and goals. These activities may be organized in the following way:

- research (fact-finding);
- strategic planning;
- service enhancement and program development; and
- promotion.

Research

Conducting surveys of important healthcare consumers and clients (i.e., patients, physicians, employers, community), keeping up-to-date on healthcare trends and opportunities, and evaluating population trends are all ways to keep the organization in touch with its environment. Marketing continuously conducts these activities in an ongoing effort to maintain communication with its clients.

Strategic planning

With the great number of opportunities that are likely to be uncovered as a result of marketing's research, it is important to have a means to select the "right" opportunities for the institution. The document that helps guide these decisions is the strategic plan, which usually provides a course for the organization to follow for five to ten years. It identifies the hospital's strengths and weaknesses, as well as market trends and opportunities, to define the organization's priorities (or strategies) for the ensuing years. While the development of this plan may or may not be coordinated by the marketing staff (many hospitals also have a separate planning department), marketing input is critical to the strategic planning process.

Service enhancement and program development

Guided by the strategic plan and the input from research activities, the marketing staff must determine the fine-tuning necessary to assure all parties that the healthcare organization is meeting its clients' demands. Staff members work with other departments to ensure that services are delivered in a manner consistent with their customers' wants. The marketing staff also looks for—and takes advantage of—opportunities for new programs that will help the organization meet the goals outlined in the strategic plan.

Promotion

Probably the most visible activity performed by the marketing staff is the promotion of the healthcare organization's services. This is the other half of the communication link that marketing provides with the organization's clients; while research "listens," promotion "speaks."

Through advertising, direct mail, educational events, and other activities, marketing actively tells its clients, "We heard what you wanted, and here it is." To send the most appropriate message in the way that will make it most likely to be heard requires that the marketing staff understand each of its target populations (i.e., the old, the young, families, ethnic groups, physicians, employers, etc.), and that they address each uniquely.

Interdepartmental Relationships

As a staff function, marketing relates to the entire organization. It is positioned to act as a resource for all departments, helping them define their particular marketing issues and needs.

A Look to the Future

In response to the rapid changes taking place, healthcare organizations will continue to turn to marketing to spearhead strategic planning that will determine their future. Specifically, marketing will be the catalyst in guiding the healthcare organization through a highly competitive market. Seeking alliances with physician groups, determining profitable strategic alliance initiatives with other healthcare providers, and introducing new health services are but a few of the responsibilities that will continue to be placed with the marketing function. Healthcare is a service business competing in the largest service industry in the United States. Unless healthcare organizations effectively market present services and strategically plan future services they will not survive term in today's competitive managed care environment.

REFERENCE

Joint Commission on Accreditation of Healthcare Organizations. 1997. *Comprehensive Accreditation Manual for Hospitals: The Effective Manual.* Chicago: JCAHO.

7

The Outside Professional

The architect, accountant, attorney, consultant, and sales representative all play an important role as members of the healthcare team, whose functions are described in this chapter. Appropriate use of these and other outside professionals is important in creating, sustaining, and improving the healthcare organization's environment. The demand for outside professionals has increased since the advent of managed care in that the use of outside expertise has proven in many instances to be more cost effective.

ARCHITECT

The architect must combine artistic skill, engineering knowledge, and a thorough familiarity with legal requirements in working with the various members of the healthcare organization's professional staff for the development of new or remodeled areas. This professional must be aware of how people react to their environment and of ways in which people and their surroundings interrelate and interact. Such a professional will help produce an environment that is not only functional but also able to promote the concepts of quality patient care and high employee morale and productivity.

The architect must also be aware of medical and scientific developments as well as possible future developments so that the facility designed today will perform adequately in the decades ahead. Planning a new facility is a joint effort of the architect and the institution staff. Together, they must consider each department's functions; the personnel performing them; functional, environmental, personnel interrelationships; and the supporting equipment and services required.

ACCOUNTANT

The business office and the management staff work closely with outside accounting or auditing firms. Often a number of auditors work with a given institution. To perform the job adequately, the auditor must have a thorough knowledge of each department's functions and of the interrelationships of departmental activities. This knowledge enables the auditor to work constructively with the entire staff in examining cost reports, controls, and procedures.

The staff should work together with the auditors for the organization's benefit. The auditors are in a position to review objectively the control functions within the institution and to note areas requiring improvement. Putting their suggestions into practice results in reducing operating costs. Auditors representing insurance companies or government agencies also perform a valuable service both for their clients and the healthcare organization in terms of adequate and justified reimbursement. Suggestions made regarding budgets, costs analysis, and productivity standards enable an organization to be more productive.

ATTORNEY

The healthcare organization's legal counsel is also an invaluable member of the healthcare team. The institution and its personnel must adhere to many legal requirements and codes. Questions involving confidentiality of information, consents, and bylaws, as well as issues involving the medical staff, licensing requirements, and malpractice actions, are just a few of the hundreds of legal questions most organizations face. The advice and representation of an attorney who is thoroughly conversant with a healthcare organization's functions and staff is an invaluable aid.

CONSULTANT

A consultant is an expert in one subject or in many areas of concern. The board of directors and administrative staff must use consultant services intelligently. The consultant, who has the advantage of objectivity and expertise, may develop a master plan for the healthcare organization, and in evaluating or planning a program, he or she may undertake a detailed study of the community's needs. The consultant's services may also be used to explore the feasibility of a new kitchen facility, for instance, or for management consultation and supervisory development, or for advice on the training and continuing education of members of the health team, or for some combination of these activities. Many excellent consulting firms are available throughout the country to offer a wide range of expertise.

The consultant's help is important in planning, design, construction, equipment, financing, operations, maintenance, security, and training. It is important to select and make intelligent use of a consultant who is both expert within his or her area and thoroughly knowledgeable about healthcare organizations.

SALES REPRESENTATIVE

A sales representative brings to the organization expert knowledge of the products he or she represents. Although mainly interested in selling a product, sales representatives also introduce new developments within their field. Sales representatives primarily interact with the purchasing agent, pharmacist, and dietitian, but they also may be referred to other departments. They should demonstrate their products as requested and, at the same time, act as fair and objective consultants on these products. As questions arise about other firms' products, the sales representative's observations, through contact with many other institutions, add valuable knowledge to the healthcare team.

The sales representative should inform and advise the administrator of new products, developments, and other items of interest that he or she has seen elsewhere. He or she should also have a thorough knowledge of healthcare organizations, their staff, and their interrelationships and should communicate effectively as a full-fledged professional member of the healthcare organization's team.

OTHER OUTSIDE PROFESSIONALS

Many others who are involved with the healthcare organization should be mentioned, including educators, government officials, key individuals from insurance companies, insurance advisers and brokers, and hundreds of others whose advice and counsel are sought by those working within the healthcare organization. The interactions of all of these individuals are vital to the development of a full and productive healthcare team.

Part III

Healthcare Management: Principles and Practices

8

Interviewing and Selecting Highly Productive Employees

T his chapter highlights the process of interviewing and selecting highly productive employees, which is one of the healthcare manager's or supervisor's most challenging tasks. Identifying the qualities of highly effective employees is the most important part of preparing for the selection interview. Preparing for and actually conducting the interview are also important. If, however, the manager or supervisor is uncertain about the specific knowledge, skills, and other qualities that they are seeking in the highly productive employee, then the interview, at best, might not be much more than a casual conversation without a purpose. Knowing what is wanted in the most qualified applicant for employment gives the selection interview its focus and purpose.

Selecting the most qualified individuals can eliminate or minimize difficulty and frustration for both the manager and employee and is the foundation of the healthcare organization's productivity and staff development efforts.

CONDUCTING THE EMPLOYMENT INTERVIEW: SELECTING THE BEST APPLICANT

The healthcare manager or supervisor is interested in getting two basic sets of information from the applicant in the employment interview. First are the essential job requirements: Does the applicant have the minimum educational, work experience, licenses, certifications, etc., that the position requires? This information should be clearly indicated on the employment application and is determined by human resources during the initial screening.

The second, and most important part of the employment interview, is determining whether the applicant—who has the basic educational and work experience qualifications—is indeed the best fit for the organization and department. This determination can best be made if the manager or supervisor is certain of the qualities he or she is looking for in the most qualified applicant and has prepared for the interview by knowing which open-ended questions he or she will ask the applicant.

Listed below are four examples of open-ended questions that the manager might ask in the employment interview that would identify certain qualities:

1. What achievements are you most proud of regarding your work and career?

   Comment: This would be a good question to ask if the interviewer were trying to determine the applicant's initiative. The question makes reference to achievements that, in most cases, require high levels of personal initiative.

2. What was the most important project that you worked on in your last job?

   Comment: This is an effective question to determine the applicant's experience in working cooperatively in teams.

3. How could you have improved the progress made in your career?

   Comment: This would be a good question to ask to determine the applicant's satisfaction with his or her progress and current situation.

4. Why should I hire you?

   Comment: This will identify many of the prospective employee's perceptions of his or her qualities and how they match the job.

PREPARING FOR THE INTERVIEW: IDENTIFYING QUALITIES OF THE HIGHLY EFFECTIVE/PRODUCTIVE HEALTHCARE EMPLOYEE

Here are a few guidelines to consider when attempting to identify the qualities (skills and competencies) of the most qualified and productive healthcare employee:

Step 1. Assemble a group of managers and nonmanagers who are familiar with the position being recruited.

Step 2. Within the group, ask "Who is the best employee that we have presently in this position?" or "Who in the past has been the best employee in the position?"

Comment: You will find that the group will readily come to a consensus regarding the name or names of current or past employees in the position who are or have been the best.

Step 3. As a group, ask and answer "What qualities (competencies and character traits) does that employee have that make him or her the best?"

Step 4. List the qualities for further discussion and reference when preparing open-ended interview questions.

Step 5. Prepare open-ended questions that will be used by the manager or supervisor during the interview.

INTERVIEWING: QUESTIONS THAT DETERMINE THE SUITABILITY OF THE APPLICANT

Each healthcare position has unique requirements, so there is no best sequence to follow, and there is no single revealing, streamlined set of open-ended interview questions. Listed below are some samples of open-ended interview questions that can be used or adapted to more effectively identify the required skills and competencies.

1. What was the date you joined your last place of employment? What was your title? What was your starting rate of pay?
2. What do you think were your most important responsibilities in that job?
3. What special knowledge and skills did you need to perform those responsibilities?
4. What decisions or difficult problems did you have to face in your last job?
5. Tell me how you reached difficult decisions about and solutions to difficult problems.
6. What achievements are you most proud of in relation to your work/ career?
7. What have you found to be most difficult in your past jobs?
8. What was the most important project that you worked on in your last job?
9. How did you feel about the workload in your last job? How did you divide your time among your major areas of responsibility?

10. How important was communication and interaction with others in your last job?
11. With what other personnel and departments did you deal? What were the difficulties you encountered there?
12. What was more important on your last job—written or oral communication? Why?

THE EMPLOYMENT INTERVIEW: A CONVERSATION WITH A PURPOSE

Interview Skills and Preparation Guidelines

Listed below are six guidelines that the healthcare manager should consider when preparing for an effective interview.

1. Know the qualities that you are searching for in the prospective employee before the interview begins.
2. Prepare open-ended questions in advance designed to identify specific qualities and characteristics of the highly productive employee.
3. Use a quiet, comfortable location for the interview. Avoid interruptions as much as possible.
4. Introduce the purpose of the interview and outline the job requirements.
5. Encourage the applicant to ask questions and let the applicant talk freely. Much good information can be obtained by what the applicant might say spontaneously and not in response to a specific question.
6. Close the interview with specific information regarding the next steps in the interview process. Remember, the applicant will be interested in what to expect.

Dos and Don'ts

The employment interview is often the first contact a prospective employee will have with your healthcare organization, so you will want the experience to be a positive one. Here are a few dos and don'ts regarding this important interview.

Do . . .

1. Plan and prepare for the interview.
2. Use a quiet, comfortable place.
3. Put the applicant at ease.
4. Be interested in the person.

5. Clearly outline the job requirements.
6. Explain the conditions of employment.
7. Explain why the position is open.
8. Encourage the applicant to ask questions.
9. Guide and control the interview.
10. Listen and let the applicant talk freely.
11. Be yourself.
12. Know when and how to close the interview.
13. Announce your decision or explain the next steps.

Don't . . .

1. Keep the applicant waiting.
2. Build false hopes or make false promises.
3. Oversell the job.
4. Interrupt the applicant during the interview.
5. Rush through the interview.
6. Repeat questions already answered on the application.
7. Develop a "canned" interview approach.
8. Ask questions not related to the job.
9. Prejudge and reflect prejudices.
10. Send applicant away with a bad taste.
11. Use a phony excuse for not selecting the applicant.

Post–Employment Interview Evaluation

The healthcare manager should ask the following kinds of questions following the employment interview and prior to the job offer to determine whether the applicant will indeed be the right choice.

Work experience and history

1. Does the applicant have the kind and amount of experience needed?
2. Did the applicant remain on past jobs for a reasonable length of time?
3. Does the applicant's record show normal growth in responsibility and earnings?
4. Does the applicant have sound reasons for leaving prior positions?
5. Does your healthcare organization offer job conditions that the applicant is seeking?
6. Does the applicant's work history indicate that he or she gets along well with others?

Professional and educational fit

1. Has the applicant achieved a desirable level of education?
2. Has the applicant assumed positions of leadership in school, social, or business activities?
3. Does the applicant's history indicate a willingness and ability to assume responsibility?
4. Does the applicant's background indicate resourcefulness, initiative, and ambition?
5. Does the applicant appear to be an emotionally and socially mature person?
6. Does the applicant express himself or herself effectively?

Interpersonal communication skills

1. Does the applicant have the ability to be self-critical and objective?
2. Does the applicant reveal personal security and confidence in manner and attitude?
3. Does the applicant have a sound estimation of his/her worth to the healthcare organization?
4. Does the applicant seem sympathetic to the problems of others?
5. Is the applicant tolerant or critical?
6. Does the applicant accept people as they are?
7. Does the applicant accept others' point of view?

Personal motivation and attitude

1. Are the applicant's ambitions and goals in line with the opportunities the healthcare organization will offer?
2. Does the applicant have a realistic view of his or her future?
3. Does the applicant seem to be the kind of person who will grow in effectiveness?
4. Does the applicant have sound reasons for wanting the position?

CONDUCTING THE LAWFUL EMPLOYMENT INTERVIEW: LEGAL CONSIDERATIONS

The past ten years have witnessed a tremendous growth in the impact of equal employment opportunity (EEO) laws on healthcare organizations. The growing number of charges of discrimination has caused government agencies charged with enforcing EEO laws and regulations to increase their staffs to handle the rapidly growing volume of complaints. Today, more than ever, healthcare managers and supervisors must have a solid understanding of what is required to comply with EEO rules and regulations.

One of the areas in which companies are most vulnerable is the employment process. The Equal Employment Opportunity Commission reports that the selection process is responsible for more charges of discrimination than any other area of employment practices. Because of this, not only human resources staff but every manager and supervisor who interviews job candidates must be aware of areas in which even apparently innocent questions, asked in good faith, can leave the organization open to costly and time-consuming discrimination charges.

Equal Employment Opportunity Laws and the Interviewer

Both federal and state laws forbid employment interviewers to ask certain kinds of questions, which essentially means that any question asked of an applicant for employment must be based on *bona fide* occupational qualifications. This means that the employment interviewer must base employment-related interview questions on job qualifications without regard to race, color, religion, gender, national origin, pregnancy or related medical condition, age, marital status, or disability.

The safest way for the healthcare manager to prepare for the employment interview from a legal standpoint is to ensure that the questions asked of the applicant are job-related and that the questions asked do not discriminate against the applicant for reasons other than job-related factors. Thus, if any job qualifications or selection standards are based on factors other than those that are job-related—even if it is not the intention of the employment interviewer—the employer has the burden of proving that the standards are significantly related to job performance.

9

Job Coaching, Performance Evaluation, and Progressive Disciplinary Action

One of the most commonly expressed desires of employees at all levels in healthcare organizations is for complete, accurate, and timely feedback on how well they are performing their jobs. Employees want a clear understanding of job expectations, how well they are expected to do the job, and how they can improve their job performance. Additionally, employees are very interested in and appreciate job performance coaching from their supervisor. Such feedback encourages employees to increase job knowledge and skills that qualify them for increased job responsibility and earning ability.

This important management function is often viewed as the more formal interaction between the employee and supervisor that occurs at scheduled times during the year, such as at the end of the employee's probationary period of employment or during the scheduled annual evaluation. Job performance evaluation and coaching should be a daily, ongoing process. Such positive and constructive feedback results in more immediate improvements in job performance and provides encouragement and reassurance to the employee.

A very important principle of job performance feedback and coaching for the manager to remember is that job performance feedback should not occur after a period of service unless job duties and performance criteria have been clearly defined. This principle is one of the main points of this chapter. By enumerating strategies on improving performance, solving conflicts, and managing difficulties, the chapter serves as an employee manual for the healthcare manager.

JOB COACHING—WHAT IS IT?

The term *coaching* is a familiar one. Most often associated with sports and athletics, coaching relates to practice, drills, exercises, conditioning, feedback on skill execution, positive reinforcement, and repetitive skill practice that improves the fundamentals. This definition also applies very directly to the job performance of healthcare employees in all disciplines. The healthcare manager or supervisor's role as coach is to ensure—as much as possible—that employees understand what is expected of them. This requires that the manager or supervisor spend sufficient time teaching, advising, demonstrating, training, and reinforcing acceptable levels of job performance—particularly during the employee's early weeks and months of employment.

Job coaching is an informal process of communication between the employee and his or her supervisor or manager. Coaching occurs on a moment-by-moment, day-to-day basis in which the manager or supervisor teaches and reinforces the job standards and expectations. This requires an investment of quality time with the employee to ensure that their most important question is answered from the first day of employment: What is expected of me in my job?

Steps to Effective Coaching

1. Define job expectations in measurable ways. Provide encouragement.
2. Provide adequate on-the-job training.
3. Give regular job performance feedback and recognition.
4. Identify job performance problems as a skill or work habit issue.
5. Ask for the employee's help in solving the problem. Don't assume ownership of the problem.
6. Tell the employee why the problem concerns you.
7. Offer help in solving the problem (training, seminars, etc.)
8. Set performance-improvement target dates with the employee.
9. Closely observe the employee's performance during the improvement period.
10. Maintain continued improvement through reinforcement and recognition.
11. If necessary, state consequences of employee's inability to demonstrate performance improvement within an agreed-upon time period.

12. Set follow-up date, meet with employee, and initiate internal staffing decision based on performance outcome.

GUIDELINES FOR ENCOURAGING POSITIVE JOB PERFORMANCE

All employees appreciate receiving ongoing feedback from their supervisor regarding how well they are doing their jobs, and they appreciate positive reinforcement of jobs done well in addition to corrective feedback on areas in which they could perform their jobs even better. Here are a few key guidelines to encourage positive job-performance improvements:

1. Focus on positive job-performance efforts.
2. Build on the job strengths and unique assets that the employee brings to the job.
3. Recognize and acknowledge job-performance improvement.
4. When coaching, break down difficult job tasks into simple, easy-to-understand ones.
5. Focus on specific contributions that the employee has made in the department or organization.
6. Treat job-related mistakes or failures as learning opportunities.
7. Give written performance-improvement plans to the employee.
8. Set follow-up dates to review job-performance improvement progress.

KEY STEPS TO IMPROVING JOB PERFORMANCE

Occasionally, employees will have difficulty performing one or more aspects of a job at a satisfactory level. This may be the case even when the manager or supervisor has invested significant time in the coaching process. Either because of a skill or initiative problem, it may appear that the employee may not be able to perform his or her job successfully. When this is the case, the healthcare manager or supervisor, in all fairness to the employee, must initiate these specific, documented steps for improving job performance:

1. Determine whether the job performance problem is related to lack of skill or whether the substandard performance is as a result of misconduct or a policy/rule violation.
2. Assess past coaching efforts. This assures managers or supervisors that they have provided the orientation, coaching, and training necessary for the employee to succeed.
3. Review past job performance and reinforce job-performance standards with employee.

4. Describe areas of job performance that require improvement.

5. Ask for the employee's views on the reason(s) why job performance does not meet the job standard(s). The important issue to address at this point is whether the employee believes there is a problem.

6. Discuss possible solutions to the job-performance problem with the employee. Encourage the employee to come up with the solution(s) to the problem as much as possible.

7. Agree to a specific written performance-improvement plan.

8. Get employee commitment to the performance-improvement plan.

9. Positively reinforce and encourage the employee. The manager's, or supervisor's, message to the employee at this point in the process is "my goal is to do everything reasonable possible to help you succeed in your job."

10. Set a follow-up date to review and reinforce positive improvements in job performance.

SOLVING THE MORE-DIFFICULT JOB-PERFORMANCE PROBLEMS

Job-performance problems come in a variety of forms, including dress and appearance, attitude and interpersonal communication and conduct, skill-based problems, attendance and punctuality, to name a few. This section specifically relates to the key steps to solving the more-difficult job-performance problems, as well as the importance of documentation and ensuring that the healthcare manager, or supervisor, is both fair with the employee, but at the same time holds him or her accountable to perform the job duties.

Steps to Solving the More-Difficult Job-Performance Problems

Step 1. Describe the job-performance problem in a friendly manner.

Step 2. Indicate to the employee why the performance problem concerns you.

Step 3. Discuss possible causes of the problem with the employee.

Note: Though it is commendable to ask about and empathize with the employee regarding the causes of the job-performance problem, the manager or supervisor is cautioned to not allow such reasons to justify substandard performance. For example, the supervisor may empathize with why an employee has missed many scheduled workdays (i.e., because of a sick spouse, child, or parent). The focus of the problem-solving discussion should not be on the reasons for absenteeism in this case but rather on that fact the employee is failing to report to work regularly and on time. In such situations, the manager or supervisor must find a balance between empathizing with the employee and at the same time reinforcing in a firm, fair, and kind way the employee's job responsibilities.

Step 4. Identify and list possible solutions to the job-performance problem.

Step 5. With the employee, decide on specific actions each of you will take to realize job-performance improvement.

Step 6. Agree to a follow-up meeting to review job-performance progress.

THE PERFORMANCE-EVALUATION INTERVIEW

Performance feedback—whether good or bad—often fuels change and always initiates communication between managers and staff. All employees deserve a clear understanding of their job expectations, how well or poorly they are performing their duties, and what they can do to improve and advance in their jobs and careers. The performance-evaluation interview is the ideal setting for answering these key employee questions.

Purposes of the Performance-Evaluation Interview

The performance-evaluation interview ideally serves to:
1. inventory the talents, skills, and career interests of the employee;
2. give the employee objective feedback on job performance, reinforce positive job performance, and offer help for job-performance improvement;
3. assist the employee in his or her career and professional-development planning; and
4. discuss compensation in relation to job performance.

The Performance-Evaluation Interview: Common Concerns

Listed below are several common concerns and dynamics that healthcare managers and supervisors often experience during the performance-evaluation process.
1. Because of the sensitivities involved with discussing an employee's job performance, the employee sometimes becomes emotional and subjective in the discussion.
2. Finding a balance between communicating positive job-performance feedback and listing areas for improvement is often difficult.

3. Those evaluated tend to take the performance feedback personally; defensiveness is common.

4. Because of #3, managers and supervisors tend to delay the performance evaluation.

5. Employees are concerned or annoyed when their scheduled performance evaluations and pay increase (when scheduled and anticipated) are delayed.

6. Performance evaluation ratings may be altered or biased for subjective reasons.

JOB COACHING, EVALUATING PERFORMANCE, AND AVOIDING EMPLOYMENT LITIGATION

It is reasonable to assume that healthcare employees who feel treated fairly are more likely to be productive and stay with employer longer. Conversely, employees who feel unfairly or unreasonably treated are more likely to be less productive, leave their employer sooner, and, most significantly, find cause to file a grievance or take some type of litigated action against the employer.

Effective job coaching and performance evaluation ensure that, to a large extent, employees are treated fairly in the following ways:

1. they are sufficiently oriented and trained in their positions;
2. they are informed on a timely basis of job-performance problems;
3. they are provided opportunities (through additional coaching and training) to improve their job performance;
4. they are informed of the consequences of their failure or inability to perform the reasonable expectations of their job; and
5. any action that would affect the employee's employment status is taken only if the employee has been thoroughly trained, informed of job-performance problems, given opportunities to improve, and has been fairly warned of the consequences of unsatisfactory job performance.

MANAGING DIFFICULT EMPLOYEE BEHAVIOR

Managing difficult employee behavior—often described as unpleasant attitudes, mood swings, and sometimes irrational conduct—is at, or near, the top of the list of unpleasant tasks that many healthcare managers and supervisors face.

Understandably, most managers and supervisors would prefer not to have to deal with such problems. The reality, however, is that for a variety of reasons there are times when the manager must seek to understand and positively influence negative employee behaviors and attitudes. Such conduct is not acceptable in the healthcare workplace; it negatively affects the morale of coworkers, it is regarded as unsatisfactory job performance, and it most often is reason enough for the manager to initiate progressive disciplinary action. The employee's responsibility in these instances is to respond willingly to the manager's fair and reasonable requests to correct these job-related behavioral problems.

Listed below are a few coaching and counseling skills that address the following assumptions regarding difficult employee behavior.

1. In most cases, there are rational reasons why employees behave negatively or unpleasantly.
2. Employees are generally unaware that their behavior is not appropriate in the workplace and appreciate being advised accordingly by their supervisor and held accountable for correcting the behavior or attitude problem.
3. In some cases, employees are not aware that their conduct on the job is negatively affecting their coworkers or their own job performance.
4. Employees, for the most part, appreciate constructive feedback from their supervisors regarding unacceptable attitudes or behaviors on the job.

Managing Difficult Employee Behavior: Key Guidelines

It is important that the healthcare manager and supervisor recognize that the management of employee behavioral problems is much more difficult, generally, than the more measurable skill-based performance problems. Therefore, significant tact and diplomacy are required to help the employee understand and accept feedback regarding how their conduct may be negatively affecting their own or their coworkers' job performance. The following suggested guidelines should be helpful to the manager or supervisor who is leading a job-performance improvement discussion with an employee regarding on-the-job behaviors that need change and improvement.

1. **Review positive aspects of past performance,** particularly as they relate to the employee's ability to interact positively with coworkers.
2. **Describe the unacceptable on-the-job behavior or conduct.** Be specific, but kind, with the employee during this sensitive part of the interview. Anticipate defensiveness from the employee and allow your responses and interactions with the employee to be supportive.
3. **Ask for employee feedback regarding the behavior problem.** Your interest is in determining whether the employee regards his or

her conduct as a performance problem and, most importantly, whether the employee will be motivated to take initiatives to correct that problem. This particular coaching exercise assumes that the employee is cooperative and receptive to coaching and advice from the manager. In this key step, the manager is seeking to understand the employee's explanation for the cause of the unacceptable behavior.

4. **Discuss possible solutions to correcting the problem**—preferably those solutions suggested by the employee that are acceptable to the manager.

5. **Agree to a performance improvement action plan** and make sure the employee commits to it.

6. **Give positive reinforcement and set a follow-up date** to review performance improvement progress with the employee.

7. **Hold the follow-up meeting** to review performance improvement progress.

Note: The steps to effective coaching for performance improvement assumes positive responses from the employee and the employee's willingness to change undesirable on-the-job behavior. Chapter 11, "Employee Motivation Skills," includes steps that the manager or supervisor can take in cases where the employee seems unwilling or unable to change unsatisfactory job performance.

PROGRESSIVE DISCIPLINARY ACTION

By accepting employment with a healthcare organization, employees agree to comply with its policies and procedures and to represent the employer's best interests. Employees are held responsible for their personal actions on the job. When an employee violates established policies or procedures, disciplinary action up to and including termination from employment may be appropriate.

Disciplinary action other than termination from employment is taken to correct an employee's poor conduct or performance, and to help the employee succeed in his or her employment relationship with the employer.

The objective of the progressive disciplinary process is to correct otherwise unacceptable conduct and behavior of employees. To discipline is not to punish. One of the main outcomes of progressive disciplinary action is that the employee be granted the opportunity by the manager to correct unacceptable on-the-job behavior and to be informed of the consequences of an inability or unwillingness to do so.

Progressive Discipline, Positive Employee Relations, and Litigation Avoidance

It is important that healthcare managers and supervisors understand and accept the idea that there is a relationship between how employees are treated by the manager in the disciplinary process and the employee's response to that process. If the employee feels harshly or unfairly treated, he or she will likely react negatively. Conversely, the employee who feels treated fairly and with respect will likely respond favorably.

The key concern here is that employees will somehow retaliate against their employer if they feel that they have reason to do so. And employees can retaliate in a number of ways. Tardiness, absenteeism, and lack of teamwork and cooperation with coworkers are but a few of these negative and costly employee responses. Further, if employees feel justified in their feelings of unfair dealing, they may exercise the organization's in-house grievance procedure and/or initiate formal litigation against the healthcare organization. Litigation, of course, is the least desirable of the two outcomes to have to manage. Defense litigation is costly and very disruptive to operations and employee relations.

Employees have the basic right to be treated with dignity and respect during any management/employee interaction, and this is particularly true during the progressive disciplinary process where feelings of defensiveness and sensitivities can be high. Applying a fair and equitable disciplinary process is important to ensure that employees are treated with dignity and respect regardless of work-related circumstances.

Administering discipline positively and progressively is literally a form of litigation avoidance and risk management by healthcare managers and supervisors. The relationship between progressive discipline and litigation avoidance should be kept in mind by the manager in all aspects of employee relations—particularly during the administration of the progressive disciplinary process.

Progressive Discipline Guidelines

Employee discipline should be considered less as punishment and more as training and self-discipline to follow certain technical procedures and specific job duties. Although there are times when it becomes necessary to administer punitive discipline such as withholding rewards, demotion, suspensions without pay, and the like, this type of discipline should be the exception rather than the rule.

What follows is a listing of progressive disciplinary guidelines that healthcare managers and supervisors can refer to and can implement as needed.

1. Focus on the undesirable job performance, not on the employee's personality or attitude.
2. Gain the employee's commitment to change, to put forth the effort to bring about a positive change in performance and/or behavior.
3. Use a positive approach and listen to feedback—let the employee tell his or her side.

4. Document all coaching, counseling, and follow-up meetings with the employee.

5. Do not procrastinate—immediately communicate job performance, attendance, safety problems, and other work-related job-performance deficiencies.

6. Follow a progressive process:
    - verbal counseling (documented)
    - second written warning
    - final written warning
    - definitive action

7. Suspensions should rarely be used and only when it is in the organization's best interest to remove the employee from the workplace, pending management investigation and final determination of the job performance problem.

Examples of employee misconduct that may be grounds for suspension include fighting, substance abuse, accident with serious endangerment to patients and employees, property damage, or gross misconduct.

Consider that each case of disciplinary action should be evaluated by the nature of the problem, severity, and the employee's overall employment history. Factors such as length of service, attendance, and past performance are part of this evaluation.

Depending on the severity of the employee's job-performance problem and his or her employment history, it may be necessary to bypass the progressive discipline move to termination of employment. Such action would be taken in situations of willful misconduct in the workplace such as theft, defacing property, gross insubordination, violence, or no-call and no-show for work.

Employee Performance Follow-Up and Continuous Counseling Process

It is important that employees understand that the intent of any level of progressive discipline is to help them to succeed in their jobs. Therefore, it is important that follow-up discussions with employees be held on a timely basis. This assures the employee that the issue is important and that the healthcare manager or supervisor is genuinely interested in helping the employee to succeed.

The following guidelines may be helpful when initiating employee performance follow-up.

1. Review previous discussions and reinforce positive changes in employee job performance or refocus on any outstanding problems or lack of progress since the previous performance management counseling session. Be specific and use examples!

2. Ask for the employee's opinion of why progress hasn't been made.

3. Discuss what solutions the employee intends to make to ensure progress. Agree to an action plan and have the employee commit to a timetable or a milestone chart.

4. Discuss what the next disciplinary steps are and what the time frame will be.

5. Reaffirm the employee's commitment and show confidence that they can succeed.

PROBLEMS OF WILLFUL MISCONDUCT VERSUS SUBSTANDARD JOB PERFORMANCE

It is important that healthcare managers understand that an employee who willfully disregards the employer's interests by his or her conduct and/or performance should receive progressive disciplinary action without hesitation. The steps in this process were outlined earlier.

Substandard or unsatisfactory job performance as determined by the healthcare manager or supervisor is not necessarily an indication that the employee is negligent or is disregarding the employer's interests. What it does mean, in most cases, is that the employee lacks the skill and/or knowledge required to raise himself or herself to a higher and satisfactory level of job performance. Disciplinary action would not be necessary in such cases.

Identifying Willful Misconduct Problems

Problems of employee willful misconduct can be defined as any act by an employee that violates established policy or procedures or disregards the employer's interests. Such conduct has been summarized previously in this chapter and is usually clearly defined in employee handbooks and/or human resource policies. It is important that healthcare managers or supervisors familiarize themselves with these policies and communicate them to all employees.

10

Time Management and Personal Productivity for Healthcare Managers and Supervisors

ncreased productivity in healthcare organizations, as well as the overall health and vitality of an organization, begins with individual productivity improvement. This is the effective use of the most valuable and limited resource—time.

Healthcare managers and supervisors are busy. The combination on today's manager or supervisor of their work and domestic demands seems at times to be overwhelming. What can the manager or supervisor do to overcome the feeling of constantly taking "one step forward and two steps back" in their professional and domestic responsibilities? Is there a relationship between effective time management and reductions in feelings of anxiety and stress? Do managers often feel that they are caught up in the thick of thin things, as the expression goes? Would they feel more energetic about their daily work and service activities if they had the feeling that they were focused on worthwhile goals rather than just doing busy work?

This chapter directly addresses these kinds of questions and emphasizes personal planning and goal setting (personal effectiveness) as well as time management skills and techniques (personal efficiency) as important aspects of increased productivity, health, and vitality of today's busy healthcare managers and supervisors.

PLANNING AND GOAL-SETTING: KEYS TO EFFECTIVE TIME MANAGEMENT AND PERSONAL PRODUCTIVITY

Planning your work and working your plan is a familiar expression for many healthcare managers and supervisors. It suggests that merely completing daily tasks from a to-do list will have no real value unless those tasks are directed toward accomplishing pre-planned and worthwhile goals. The busy manager often feels that most of his or her time is spent "fighting fires"—reacting to situations and circumstances that are unplanned and unexpected from day to day. This is acceptable—to an extent. Healthcare managers and supervisors must be flexible enough to respond to certain unexpected problems and even emergencies that occur from time to time. If the manager seldom finds the time to work on pre-planned goals and priorities that have high value to him or her, however, he or she will begin to feel frustrated and victimized by the priorities and needs of others. What, then, must managers or supervisors do to increase their personal effectiveness and productivity and begin to more effectively manage their time? Plan and set goals!

A Planning and Goal-Setting Exercise: Planning Your Work and Working Your Plan

A little time each day spent planning your work and setting goals and priorities will result in increased personal productivity, satisfaction, and value to you and your healthcare organization. Here is a simple exercise that invites you to define a goal, a statement of intent with a high value both to you and your employer. In this exercise, list four work-related goals that you would like to accomplish. For each goal, be as specific as you can and indicate by when you expect to accomplish it.

Goal: *Target Completion Date:*

1. _____   _____

2. _____   _____

3. _____   _____

4. _____   _____

5. _____   _____

6. _____   _____

MAXIMIZING USE OF TIME: CONTROLLING INTERRUPTIONS AND OTHER TIME WASTERS

Without question, personal discipline is necessary to succeed in accomplishing pre-established goals. In the previous exercise, you listed several goals that you would like to achieve. We defined those goals as statements of intent that with a high value both to you and your employer. The real test of the healthcare manager's regard for that value will be demonstrated by the discipline of effectively managing time, which, in part, means controlling interruptions and other time wasters. It is helpful for the effective time manager occasionally to take an inventory of time wasters and other time management issues.

Reader Exercise: Maximizing Utilization of Time

This exercise's purpose is to encourage readers to reflect on a variety of issues pertaining to effective time use. The reader is encouraged to complete the sentences that follow. There are no right or wrong answers. You should reflect on high-priority tasks or goals, time wasters, and what you can do to control them.

1. Time is . . .
2. I use time well when I . . .
3. I feel that I waste time when . . .
4. A high-priority task for me is . . .
5. A low-priority task for me is . . .
6. When I waste time I feel . . .
7. Others waste my time when . . .
8. I waste the time of others when . . .
9. I could increase my personal productivity by eliminating the unnecessary task(s) of . . .
10. My most effective time management technique is . . .
11. I put off doing important tasks that I should do when . . .
12. My image of myself as a time manager is . . .
13. The task(s) I enjoy most in my work is . . .
14. Aspects of my work that could be simplified are . . .

As a result of this exercise, you should have identified what tends to interfere with the timely achievement of high-priority goals and priorities and determined what you can do to control the time wasters—and this will result in more effective time management.

TIME MANAGEMENT SKILLS AND INSIGHTS: INCREASING PERSONAL EFFECTIVENESS, EFFICIENCY, AND ACHIEVEMENT

The principles and skills of effective time management are fairly basic and easy to understand. Some of the most common are listed below. Consistently applying these principles and skills will result in higher levels of personal productivity and satisfaction for healthcare managers and supervisors.

Review the following time management insights and skills. Include others you know of but that may not be listed in this exercise. The focus of the exercise is to reinforce time management principles and skills that can benefit healthcare managers and supervisors.

1. Use a time management tool for recording daily tasks and schedules.
2. Handle each piece of paper only once and do something with it.
3. Work from a clean desk top or work area. This will eliminate distractions.
4. Take some time each day to plan and organize work priorities.
5. Recognize procrastination behavior and work to eliminate this behavior.
6. Be aware of "time robbers" and know how to avoid and or manage them.
7. Make a point of doing at least one thing very well each day.
8. Reward yourself for accomplishing daily tasks and goals.
9. Be focused and flexible in your work.
10. Write your daily tasks (to-do list) in one place and keep it with you.
11. Ask "What am I doing right now that someone else can be doing for me?" Delegate as much as possible.
12. Do not hesitate to expect privacy when necessary to accomplish high-priority tasks. This will require discipline on your part.
13. Develop the ability to concentrate on high-priority tasks despite distractions and the natural tendency to procrastinate.
14. Ask these questions frequently regarding your work: Am I doing things right? (efficiency focus) and Am I doing the right things? (effectiveness focus).
15. Always have something to read with you. Advance on your reading during those unexpected free moments at the airport, doctor's office, etc.

11

Employee Motivation Skills

Healthcare managers and supervisors are in positions of influence—leadership positions with responsibility for creating and maintaining work environments in which employees can work cooperatively and productively as members of teams. Effective healthcare managers or supervisors realize that their success as leaders is largely based on the ability to build and maintain positive working relationships with employees. Motivated and productive employees are loyal employees, who exercise high levels of work initiative and willingly solve work-related problems. They have a positive outlook toward customers and employee relations and are genuinely interested in improving the quality of services being delivered to all customers.

This chapter emphasizes several significant aspects of employee morale, attitudes, and motivation and provides practical information related to the following questions: How can the busy healthcare manager or supervisor create and sustain high levels of personal, physical, and mental energy when dealing with numerous work-related problems and difficult situations? How does the manager or supervisor influence or create a positive work environment for employees? What can managers or supervisors do to help their employees become self-motivated and more productive on the job? These are common but difficult management questions.

It should be emphasized as part of this chapter introduction that the subjects of employee morale, attitudes, and motivation have been presented and written about over the years often with a heavy emphasis on theory. We instead emphasize the practical skills and principles of these important management subjects.

EMPLOYEE MOTIVATION AND PRODUCTIVITY IN HEALTHCARE ORGANIZATIONS

Employee motivation and productivity are influenced by a number of factors, the most significant of which is the influence of leaders (positive and negative) at all levels within healthcare organizations. Another way of viewing the general subject of employee motivation is within the context of employee work habits or job performance and workplace behavior. Employee work habits (behavior) can be categorized as either asset or liability behavior—again, influenced significantly by their managers and supervisors. Examples of asset/liability behavior are noted in Table 11.1.

For the most part, the asset behavior of employees is influenced and maintained by leaders and managers who deal with people effectively. Personal experience has demonstrated to many managers that there is a striking relationship between leader effectiveness and positive employee morale, service/product quality and—ultimately—the financial bottom line in healthcare organizations. The issue of organizationwide employee motivation and morale is largely an issue of management and leadership influence of employees.

Recognition, appreciation for good work, opportunities for growth, challenging work, responsibility, and participation in decision making are the traditional motivators that need to be internalized and become an integral part of one's management style to maintain and increase the employee's asset behaviors (positive morale).

Table 11.1 Asset/Liability Behavior

Asset Employee Behaviors	Liability Employee Behaviors
Punctual	Tardy
Subordinate	Insubordinate
Willingly participates	Seldom participates
Asks questions	Does not ask questions
Volunteers to help	Waits to be asked or told
Compliments others	Criticizes others
Seldomly complains	Frequently complains
Education continues	Education stops
Seeks responsibility	Avoids responsibility
Doesn't expect rewards until later	Expects rewards first
Solves problems	Avoids problems

EMPLOYEE MOTIVATION SKILLS: GUIDELINES FOR HEALTHCARE MANAGERS AND SUPERVISORS

Much of the literature on the subject of employee motivation implies that managers and supervisors cannot directly cause employees to be motivated. Rather, because of their positions of influence, they are more successful at indirectly creating positive work environments within which employees will more likely become more motivated—that is, becoming more enthusiastic toward work itself and their work associates, showing increased loyalty to the healthcare organization, exercising higher levels of initiative, and cooperating more fully in work involving other members of their team.

The following principles, if followed by healthcare managers and supervisors, will likely result in a more positive influence on subordinate employees and higher levels of employee motivation.

As a healthcare manager or supervisor,

1. I understand the importance of high levels of trust in working relationships. More importantly, I am committed to learning and applying the skills and habits necessary to establish a trustworthy nature to promote harmony and teamwork among my healthcare team.
2. I acknowledge and accept the responsibility to be a source of positive influence to coworkers and to be professional and fair in supporting organizational policies, regardless of circumstances.
3. I believe that setting goals cooperatively supported by all employees involved is an important management function and is essential to overall management effectiveness within my healthcare organization.
4. I will consistently strive to promote initiative at the highest levels among my employees.
5. I always strive to project a positive attitude. Occasionally, negative feelings and frustrations dominate my thinking momentarily. I understand the principles of a proactive nature—namely, that I can control and choose a more favorable response to any given circumstance. Unlike Newton's third law of motion, the law of positive interpersonal relations suggests that for most human reactions there should not be an equal and opposite reaction.
6. I am committed to instilling confidence in my employees at all times.
7. I will maintain positive and acceptable levels of motivation and energy in my managerial and supervisory roles. Much of my energy comes from staying focused on important high-priority tasks.

Overview of Employee Motivation

Motivation comes from the word *motivate*, which in turn is derived from the Latin word *movere*, "to move." Motivation, then, is anything that moves an employee to perform. We are not defining good or bad motivation here, we are merely saying that, regardless of the reason (fear, money, recognition, achievement, etc.), a person is motivated if he or she is trying to perform.

Desire versus motivation

Desire means wanting to do something, not actually doing it. There are many who want to perform a task but, for some reason, never get around to completing it. Therefore, there is a big difference between desire and motivation. Motivation is that which actually moves a person toward the goal of doing a job, not just that which makes him or her want or desire to do a job.

Factors that Motivate Healthcare Employees to Perform at a High Level

For healthcare employees to perform at a high level, the environment must allow them to gain a sense of achievement in accomplishing their jobs. It is generally agreed that most people want to do a good job. This is an expression of feeling that "I am important and my contributions are important to the company effort." When employees feel they are contributing and that they are productive, they will realize a sense of achievement.

Healthcare leaders have at their disposal certain tools they can use to create an environment where employees will motivate themselves to do a good job. These tools, called motivators, are:

1. achievement;
2. recognition;
3. participation; and
4. opportunity for growth.

If healthcare employees work at a job that allows them a sense of achievement, and the leader and employee together see the value and importance of the work to be performed, the employee will feel productive.

If employees attain a high level of performance and are recognized by their leader or their coworkers for doing a good job, this should encourage them to continue their efforts.

If employees are motivated by participation, they can help establish work goals or actually plan the work to be accomplished.

If employees see that their job will lead to their individual growth and overall job knowledge, their performance should be positively affected.

HEALTHCARE MANAGERS AND SUPERVISORS AS PERSONAL MOTIVATORS AND POSITIVE INFLUENCE

A key consideration regarding employee motivation relates to the energy level and positive influence healthcare managers and supervisors can have. Because they are in positions of influence, their influence affects employee morale. Employee morale affects service quality, and service quality ultimately affects facility operations and the organization's financial bottom line.

How, then, can the healthcare manager or supervisor maintain and increase his or her personal levels of motivation and energy? Listed below are a few personal motivation suggestions:

1. Always focus on your personal strengths, talents, and uniqueness. Keep self-talk positive.
2. Look for and highlight the positive aspects of your present conditions or circumstances. Concentrate on improving your circumstances—whatever they may be.
3. Do something every day to enhance your relationship with someone else in your personal and professional life.
4. Maintain an ongoing program of continuing self-development.
5. Set and achieve worthwhile goals. Reward yourself for successful goal achievement.
6. Reward yourself regularly for jobs well done and goals achieved.

12

Customer Service Skills for Healthcare Managers

C ustomer service compliments and complaints indicate that there is a strong relationship among leadership effectiveness, positive employee relations, and service excellence in healthcare organizations. This is an important dynamic that must be understood and practiced in order to remain highly competitive in an already competitive industry in which the customer has clearly made known an increasing demand for service quality.

Quality customer service is not presented here as a topic that is new to the health service industry. Rather, service delivery is presented as the "quality" aspect of employee job performance—a significant dimension of job performance for which employees at all levels of a healthcare organization should be held accountable.

The healthcare business is the premier people business. Highly skilled and often labor-intensive healthcare organizations and departments deal regularly with very sensitive and emotional issues that people experience as patients. Service professionals must be sensitive to a wide range of human emotion the customer feels and often expresses. Common courtesy, active listening, a professional demeanor, and the ability and willingness to empathize with the customer are but a few of the qualities and skills required of health service providers.

Positive employee relations and service quality will be emphasized in this chapter, as well as the importance of positive communication, service perception, first impressions, meeting customer expectations, managing the difficult customer, and customer service performance accountability.

POSITIVE COMMUNICATIONS AND SERVICE MARKETING IN HEALTHCARE ORGANIZATIONS

Positive communication means uplifting, enthusiastic, caring, and assuring communication to the customer. It means affirmative responses to customer requests and questions that they may have regarding any aspect of the health services that they are receiving. Positive communication by health service providers strengthens the relationship between the customer and the service organization. Positive communication is conveyed both verbally as well as nonverbally in many ways. It sends the message that we "sincerely care" and have an interest in your welfare, concerns, and problems.

The messages communicated to health service customers are often interpreted in only one of two ways—positive or negative. Interestingly enough, and of major significance to service providers, is that customers act as "marketing agents" for the organization. What they say to their family, friends, work associates, and neighbors regarding the quality of services received are based largely on the nature of the communication between themselves and those representing the healthcare organization. Further, what they communicate can be dramatically positive or negative depending on how they feel they were treated by the staff. This is a bottom-line issue.

Perception, First Impression, and Customer Service in Healthcare Organizations

An understanding of perception and the power of first impression is of major significance to healthcare providers intent on delivering the quality of service that the customer has a right to expect from today's healthcare organizations.

We define perception as "becoming aware of something through sight, hearing, touch, taste, or smell." We form some of our strongest opinions and viewpoints about the world around us based on our perception. Our perception of things as they are may have little to do with facts or what actually happened. This is particularly significant as it relates to the customer services a healthcare organization provides.

We define first impression as "having an effect on our mind or emotions." The manner in which health services are provided to the customer (i.e., patient, family member, etc.), regardless of the sophistication of technique or technology required to provide the service, will often have an immediate and lasting effect on the customer's mind or emotions. The mannerism, cordiality, common courtesy, and positive consideration for what the customer may be thinking or feeling while receiving services is of paramount importance.

TEN CONSIDERATIONS FOR HEALTH SERVICE EXCELLENCE

Listed below are ten key actions that can result in health service excellence. Review each and evaluate the application of the practice in your department or service area. Consider specifically what prevents any of the following and how you can overcome any of the barriers to quality customer service.

1. Greet the customer with a friendly smile.
2. Give the customer your undivided attention.
3. Acknowledge the customer's presence during busy moments with other customers.
4. Be sincere. Listen and respond courteously and with empathy.
5. Be energetic and cordial.
6. Be the customer's agent. Take ownership of their questions or concerns.
7. Bend the rules or policy occasionally to the customer's benefit.
8. Offer assistance and help regularly.
9. Be prompt in your response to the customer.
10. Thank the customer for the opportunity to be of service.

MANAGING THE DIFFICULT CUSTOMER

The customer may not always be right. In fact, there are times when the customer may be downright rude and offensive. This makes dealing positively with him or her very difficult—at best—for the healthcare professional. However, it is not the nature of customers to be short-tempered and difficult to deal with in the healthcare setting. With rare exception, patients receiving health services are cordial and understanding and appreciate the care they are given.

For healthcare professionals to cope most effectively with and manage difficult customers, they must be able to empathize with the customer (i.e., patient)—to see the world of health services through their eyes at the time that they are receiving care. What are they feeling and experiencing? What difficult situations are they dealing with at the time of service? How long has it been since they were in a healthcare organization such as a hospital? What are their real worries and concerns? Are they feeling uncertain and insecure about the care that they will be receiving? What can I, as the service provider, do to alleviate some of these very real worries and concerns?

These are important questions that the effective health service provider must ask at all times. Additionally, it is important that healthcare providers realize that customer behavior is caused—there is usually a rational reason why customers sometimes act in unpleasant ways. The service provider cannot take such behavior personally. His or her job is to seek to understand what the customer is concerned about, empathize with the customer, and go about solving the complaint in a timely and courteous manner.

THE PROS AND CONS OF ASKING ABOUT SERVICE

A fair assumption is that regularly asking the customer "Are you getting good service?" is a valuable and important practice in any service organization, and there are many obvious advantages that result from such a customer-service approach. Conversely, this key customer-oriented question is too often not asked of the customer at the time that services are being rendered. Why? This exercise is designed to clarify answers to that question.

List below both the advantages and disadvantages, if any, of regularly asking the customer about service. Discuss particularly what the healthcare professional can do to overcome any hesitancy to ask this important question of the customer during routine courses of delivering services.

Advantages (pros)	Disadvantages (cons)— if any
1. _____	_____
2. _____	_____
3. _____	_____
4. _____	_____
5. _____	_____
6. _____	_____

CUSTOMER SERVICE QUALITY STANDARDS

Healthcare customers define service quality in nontechnical terms. For example, to many customers, quality health services include common courtesy, response time, dress and appearance of health services personnel, parking conveniences, etc. Conversely, healthcare professionals often define quality in highly technical terms—terms that patients often do not understand.

As an exercise, list below those factors that the customer (i.e., patient) might consider as a standard or standards of service excellence as they pertain to your particular health service area. Be specific regarding measurement of such standards. Then, identify those quality service standards that can be considered universal throughout the healthcare organization.

Department Service Standard	Universal Service Standard
1. _____	_____
2. _____	_____
3. _____	_____
4. _____	_____
5. _____	_____
6. _____	_____

CONTINUOUS CUSTOMER SERVICE IMPROVEMENT

Improvements in customer service quality should be an ongoing function of every health service provider. It is important for healthcare professionals to accept the notion that there is a direct relationship between quality customer service and the financial bottom line.

List below at least six significant improvements in customer service that can be implemented in your organization or department. Think in terms of service quality as defined by the customer.

Customer Service Improvement	Benefits
1. _____	_____
2. _____	_____
3. _____	_____
4. _____	_____
5. _____	_____
6. _____	_____

Part IV

Automation in the Healthcare Organization

13

Information Systems Applications

Managed care and healthcare organization integration has placed enormous pressure on information systems. The need for cost data, as well as the integration of data from the various components of integrated systems, has placed many demands on systems technology and personnel. A healthcare provider (e.g., an HMO) is at a distinct disadvantage if it cannot completely analyze the cost of delivery when dealing with an insurer. Similarly, an inability to integrate patient data across a system will produce increased costs and inefficiencies. This chapter outlines the various components—business services, pharmacy, medical records, to name a few—that have received attention and are continually being analyzed for further improvement.

The role of computers in healthcare organizations has changed rapidly, as it has in many service organizations. The words used to describe information systems reflect that changing role. The role of computers was first described as data processing because computers first served to store, manipulate, and retrieve data such as charges for services more easily and quickly. While this made functions, such as billing, more efficient, it did not help managers make complex decisions, such as how much to budget for services. Managers began asking for—and getting—more sophisticated computer programs that could help them make decisions. These more advanced systems were called management information systems. As computers became more powerful and thus capable of more complex operations, it became possible to think about creating new services with them or greatly improving existing services. Airlines created reservations systems that encouraged customers to use them because of the superior service they provided. These innovations are considered strategic uses of information systems because they help an organization to compete or to achieve its goals—or often usually both.

Hospitals and other healthcare organizations began to ask whether computers could serve the same function for them. Many hospitals, for example, offer their physicians the opportunity to connect to the hospital's computer so that they can get faster and easier access to the information they need for billing and patient care.

BUSINESS SERVICES

Within a healthcare organization, the computer's first and most common application is to the business services. As the need to handle extensive cost information for management use and reimbursement purposes has grown, the use of the computer in this area has become extensive.

The first major application for business services involves processing patients' charges. Information on patient fees can be used in various ways. First, the data collected from the patient's ledger, from the original admission data through the final charge, enable the computer to produce the patient's bill. Regardless of whether the bill is printed for the patient or on a special form for billing the third-party payor, the efficiency and speed of doing all billing by computer has been well-established in the healthcare organization, as in other businesses. Various accounts receivable reports are also possible as a by-product of the patient charging system. An aged trial balance, indicating the sources of expected revenue (from the patient, Blue Cross, or Medicare, for example) and totaled by the date of the patient's discharge, enables management to determine any payment delays.

Paying bills for supplies and keeping an accurate record of these items are also performed more efficiently through information systems. A comprehensive system includes storage of all inventories, such as those of the storeroom, pharmacy, food, and linen, on a file maintained on the computer. Items withdrawn from the inventory are noted on the appropriate file. The computer can indicate for the purchasing agent or materials manager when the item needs to be reordered, or it can print a purchase order in the required amount to be sent to the purchasing department for bidding and placing the order. Some systems can even transmit an order directly to the vendor via a modem. Confirmation and the date of shipment are then transmitted back. Keeping track of open purchase orders and indicating delays in shipments beyond a reasonable period are other potential applications.

Another major application is payroll. Information from the employees' time cards, which indicates hours worked, sick time, vacation time, and other paid and unpaid absences, is entered into the computer. Processing this information results in the employee's paycheck, together with a record of deductions. At the same time, the technology allows for preparation of payroll journals. A more sophisticated payroll system correlates this information with personnel controls. For example, such items as sick and vacation time would automatically be accumulated on the employees' file, and deductions would be made directly on that file. When the time allowed has been used, extra time is recorded as unpaid time, and the check is printed accordingly. Reports can be prepared for use by department directors and supervisors, indicating employees' absences, paid vacation and sick time remaining, and other items of value to management.

Inherent in the above systems is cost analysis and budget control. Because the accounts payable system controls and accounts for inventory, the appropriate department can be charged for each expenditure as checks are written to pay vendors for supplies. The process is the same with the payroll system: Employees' salaries can be charged to the appropriate department and section. Charges to patients can be accumulated as credit for the various departments' accounts. At the same time, units of service expressed through charges—such as laboratory determinations or respiratory therapy procedures—may be itemized as a useful management tool in determining the need for additional personnel or equipment. Based on current and accumulated information, a budget projection can be prepared by comparing actual revenue and expenditures with the proposed budget for the month and for the year-to-date; an updated projected budget on a quarterly, monthly, or even daily basis can also be furnished. Depending on the information entered into the computer at the time of admission or during the stay of the patient, it is possible to generate a wide variety of other reports.

NURSING

The use of input/output devices at the nursing station, as well as at the patient's bedside, has provided a number of applications that help reduce the amount of paperwork required by nursing personnel. All orders specified by physicians for their patients may be entered into the computer. These orders include the patient's name or identification number, the procedure or treatment ordered, and the time treatment is to be given. The orders are immediately transmitted by the computer to the various service areas. For example, all physicians' orders for x-ray films can be printed out or retrieved through a terminal in radiology, indicating the procedure, patient's unit, and other pertinent information. This enables radiology to plan the day's procedures efficiently, including scheduling of rooms and staff, and to allow for efficient transportation of the patient to the department. After the x-ray procedure has been performed, radiology enters the information into the computer, which in turn updates information in the patient's ledger. Information can then be directed back to either the nursing station terminal or directly to the patient's record, indicating that the x-ray procedure was not only performed but that its results were recorded. This same type of application is possible for all other service areas such as laboratory, physical therapy, respiratory therapy, and electrocardiography.

By processing information on the nurse's observations, patient's condition, procedures given in the unit, and various treatments and drugs given in the last eight-hour shift (and those to be given in the next eight-hour shift), a nurse can then make a change-of-shift report, using a computer terminal at his or her station or at the bedside. This report, which aids in carrying out the physician's orders, also provides a logical scheduling of patient procedures for the use of nursing personnel on the unit. Such a comprehensive report would also show any conflicts in the patient's routine, such as scheduling medication at a time that interferes with a laboratory request; this type of conflict could then be referred to the attending physician for any modification of orders.

This discussion of the possible applications of information systems to the nursing station includes only a few examples that apply to a few departments. Each application has a bearing on other applications throughout the healthcare organization. Proper patient scheduling and the appearance of this schedule in a printout or on the terminal screens at the nurses' station have an important effect on many other departments. Information systems applications on the nursing floor affect, for example, the charge data and the management report concerning units of service, and they affect the medical record itself.

PHARMACY

As all medication orders for patients on each unit are processed through the nursing station terminal(s), several advantages become apparent in this application of hospital information systems. One of the most obvious advantages is the ability to enter back through the network of nursing station terminals a medication schedule for each four- to six-hour period. Other advantages in a more sophisticated system include recording in the patient's records as well as automatically charging for drugs and automatic drug inventory.

Some pharmacy systems include such information as proper route of drug administration (i.e., oral, intravenous, intramuscular, and so forth), maximum normal dosages, compatibility of one drug with another, a patient's allergic reactions to a drug, and other pertinent drug information that can indicate any potential problems when combined with the data from the medication order. All of this can reduce—or prevent—medication errors. This information may be printed out or reviewed on a terminal for the pharmacist filling the order. To help alleviate a manual repetitive task, medication labels can be printed out through the computer terminal in the pharmacy. The pharmacy inventory can automatically be kept up-to-date, and all associated items such as the time to reorder drugs can be indicated to the pharmacist. The stock on hand at the beginning of the week, use of the stock by patient unit, and the stock on hand at the end of the week can be printed out for the pharmacy to use. The computer can also process data for determining floor stock needs and replenishment.

LABORATORY

In recent years, the laboratory has become increasingly automated. Much of the laboratory equipment enables technicians to perform many tests at the same time. In a number of sophisticated laboratories, the results of these determinations are automatically entered into a laboratory computer, which increases speed and accuracy and enables a quality control program to be instituted. The exchange of data between the laboratory system and the central hospital information system makes a number of other applications possible. Requisitions from the patient unit or outpatient department for laboratory determinations enable the laboratory to arrange for the collection of specimens and for filling the physician's orders, with the results sent back to the patient unit. Using the central hospital information system to send results back to the nursing station terminal(s) speeds delivery of the necessary information. The results of laboratory examinations can be summarized every day, week, or month for each patient. Usually, a full report in each patient unit is printed out each day. A concise report of all laboratory determinations for each patient can also be printed out daily for review by the patient's physician. It is also possible to enter the results directly into the patient's record.

RADIOLOGY

Using the computer to process a physician's order for an x-ray procedure from the nurses' station has many advantages, as has already been discussed. The computer can indicate when it is possible to schedule a particular x-ray procedure so that the nurse can prepare the patient for transportation to radiology at the appropriate time. It is also possible to determine staffing patterns within radiology by analyzing the requested procedures. The results of each x-ray examination can be processed and reported as soon as the radiologist has dictated a report. This provides rapid response to the attending physician on the patient's unit as well as valuable information for the patient's record.

OPERATING ROOM

The efficient use of available operating room time is a serious concern in many hospitals. Proper scheduling for both inpatient and outpatient surgery, based on various complex factors, can be aided through the use of hospital information systems. If a computer can process the data on the different procedures and surgeons, the most efficient use of time in the operating room obviously becomes possible. A daily report of operations to be performed, including the patient's name, type of procedure, time, and surgeon's name, can be printed out each day for use by anesthesiology and by nursing (in preparing the patient), and for other purposes such as review by the chiefs of the medical and surgical services. Anesthesiology can more easily schedule anesthesiologists and nurse anesthetists and can arrange for the proper equipment and gases to be used. Information processed by computer can also provide a number of useful management reports.

FOOD AND NUTRITIONAL SERVICES

The computer has become a valuable tool for food and nutritional services, primarily in handling the problems of selective menus and special diets. By looking at the hospital's admission, discharge, and transfer system, food and nutritional services can reduce waste. Only needed meals are sent, and those to the correct rooms. The nurse can have diet orders processed at the nurses' station, with the output appearing onscreen in the food and nutritional services office. The patient's menu selection can be processed by computer to determine raw food requirements, number of portions of each selection by patient unit, and special diets. The computer can provide a cost analysis for raw food, and personnel costs can be grouped by patients' meals, the employees' cafeteria, and the coffee shop. Information systems can also provide a dietary inventory, an accounts payable system, cost and budget control, and notification of reorder points. In addition, the scheduling of employees in food and nutritional services can be determined by analyzing the information entered into the computer.

MAINTENANCE AND ENVIRONMENTAL SERVICES

The list of potential applications of information systems to the maintenance and environmental services departments includes schedules, reports, inventories, and cost analysis. Information on schedules for preceding months, including work completed and work not completed, can indicate the work required during the next month. Such information also aids in determining proper staffing and indicates the demands on the department. Nonroutine items can also be reported in the same fashion, including a report for the preceding month, a list of the non-routine work completed during the current month, and a list of nonroutine items that are yet to be completed. A report on general scheduling can be made available at least once a month, whereas it is preferable to list nonroutine work each day. Staffing reports on a weekly basis can indicate not only the work to be done but also when it should be done and by whom. The cost analysis can indicate the effect on the budget of specific projects within the department.

The environmental services and maintenance departments are typical of many within the healthcare organization that can benefit from applying the computer to scheduling and costs. Its speedy provision of total available information can aid in the efficient use of staff, highlight any possible problems, and provide a great benefit in the constant job of keeping up-to-date on costs and understanding the meaning behind them. When new pieces of equipment are to be presented for consideration by various manufacturers and suppliers, the time necessary to do the job without the equipment can be obtained instantaneously from these computer reports, and a rapid cost analysis of the old system versus the new can be obtained. Such a quick and efficient analysis saves management time and helps managers make more knowledgeable decisions than were possible before the age of computer technology.

Introducing systems applications to preventive maintenance is one further use of the computer worth mentioning within the maintenance department. Given the many pieces of sophisticated and costly equipment, such as air-conditioning, boilers, and electronic monitoring equipment, the need for preventive maintenance is imperative so that this equipment can function efficiently for as long as possible. The computer can list all of this equipment, the frequency and type of preventive maintenance necessary, and the scheduling of this maintenance.

ADMISSION SCHEDULING

Another logical application for the computer is in admission scheduling for both inpatients and outpatients. Proper utilization of the healthcare organization demands an efficient admission system to treat the greatest number of patients consistent with the available resources. This efficiency, in turn, has great bearing on the organization's financial aspects. Whether the facility is organized to diagnose or treat patients' conditions on an ambulatory or an inpatient basis, the need for an efficient and accurate admission system is of major importance.

Many variables govern admissions to any facility. The number of beds available is easy to determine. The anticipation of a patient's discharge with as much notice as possible is important for scheduling admission of new patients. In the clinic or outpatient facility, the number of examining rooms, doctors, and other personnel is another consideration that limits the number of patients who can be seen. The length of time per examination and procedure makes the problem more complex. The type of laboratory work that might be done while the patient is in the outpatient area, as well as the time and personnel required for x-ray procedures, visits to the dietitian, sessions with the social worker, or even a minor operation, all affect scheduling. If the patient is to be admitted to a surgical unit and scheduled for surgery, the admission should be correlated with the operating room schedule. If the many factors associated with the patient's stay are considered and analyzed, the scheduling system can be a highly sophisticated one. The computer is ideally suited for manipulating the known variables and projecting the unknown variables to provide:

- a list of patients to be admitted as outpatients or to a bed inside the hospital, including preadmission information that is known (such as address, age, sex, and insurance coverage);
- the operating room schedule in correlation with the admission system; and
- a list for the use of food and nutritional services, environmental services, and other paramedical departments; for the medical staff; for anesthesiology, laboratory, and radiology; and for all other departments with schedules that are determined by the day's admission schedule.

All of these information systems applications affect many others. Reporting functions for a systems application might include listing the number of patients admitted during a given period or the number of patients seen in each outpatient area, noting diagnostic information, grouping the admissions waiting list by diagnosis and operative information as well as by category of admission (e.g., emergency, urgent, and elective), and generating many other reports for the medical staff, board of directors, and administration.

MEDICAL RECORDS

All healthcare organizations must maintain medical records, which must be both documented accurately and accessible for ready retrieval and compilation of information. The Joint Commission further requires that an accurate medical record be maintained for every person admitted as an inpatient, outpatient, or emergency patient. It is imperative that this most useful document be maintained both to be readily used while the patient is undergoing diagnosis or treatment and to furnish at a later date any necessary documentary evidence concerning the patient's illness and treatment. The medical record also serves as a basis for review and evaluation of this episode of care for the purpose of research and education.

The most common application of information systems in medical records is to the disease and operation indexes. These indexes indicate the diagnosis at the time of admission and again at the patient's discharge, and the operative procedures used. The indexes provide a quick method of reference for given diseases and operations. The requirement to maintain these indexes is well established, and all healthcare organizations have some type of index that fulfills this purpose. The indexes often are laboriously coded, compiled, and manually typewritten on a periodic basis. A hospital information system is ideally equipped to accept this coding and to print out the required indexes regularly.

By correlating this information with admission and financial data, great varieties of useful reports can be obtained. For example, the disease categories can be correlated with the many items of information on the admission file, such as age, sex, and religion.

OTHER DEPARTMENTS

The foregoing discussion represents only several of the important computer systems applications to be considered in processing information within and for a healthcare organizaiton. The list is almost endless; an information system can aid every department and section. Applying computer technology to administration is not discussed separately here because the implication of management reporting is apparent throughout each application. Storing and retrieving cost information, budget data (on a fixed and variable basis), information units of service and projections, demographic information for planning purposes, data on staffing trends and patterns, and data on performance standards for employees are made more concise and efficient through use of a complete management information system.

Use of clinical diagnostic and procedural information and detailed charge data can greatly facilitate all areas of case management. The need to maintain case data by length of stay, diagnosis (through a DRG), and physician is obvious as the institution attempts to manage its resources and produce an efficient and effective environment.

Utilization management, which is concerned with appropriate scheduling for all diagnostic and treatment procedures, enables the patient to be discharged as soon as possible; it is greatly aided by computerization.

Many physicians' offices have also become computerized and are often linked to a healthcare organization's computer. Often undertaken to increase physician loyalty, this linkage also provides the healthcare organization a marketing advantage. An information system in the physician's office can be used as a management tool for scheduling appointments, administering billings and receivables, and providing online inquiry capabilities for patient insurance information, test results, schedules, and patient status.

Entire systems have been developed and are used to interpret examination results and to print them in an understandable form for reports. For example, electrocardiographic examination results can be delivered through a telephone line with a modem as well as directly from a monitoring device that is attached to a computer. The application of the computer to many blood chemistry determinations in the hospital laboratory has been well established. The medical library has been vastly aided by computer applications in indexing and abstracting articles and books. Information systems have helped make available to the physician and student entire bibliographies in all of the medical and paramedical fields. Information systems have also eased methods of raising charitable contributions for capital and operational expenses. Other departments aided by computer applications include social services, laundry, and transportation. The future promises much more in the area of computer applications and advanced technology.

INTERNAL COMPUTER NETWORKS: INTRANETS AND INTRANET SERVICES

Healthcare organizations, integrated delivery systems, and individual facilities have come to adopt these internal networks to varying degrees. An intranet portends a similar revolution to that of the Internet in information processing. Several distinguishing features of intranets are:

- their use of computer protocols for both wide-area and local-area transport of information;
- their use of graphics, mail transport protocols, and other open Internet-based standards as the means for moving information from users to computers;
- they are completely owned by the organization and are not accessible from the Internet-at-large by the general public; and
- they are managed by information services personnel with a similar set of tools and procedures as were used to manage earlier internal networks.

While designing an intranet to meet the needs of both the healthcare organization and the consumer will obviously vary from one organization to another, the following description is typical: First, careful consideration is given to permit two levels of access—one to the staff and employees and the other to the public—in such a way as to enable relatively open communication with the public while at once providing a more secure layer for more sensitive staff communications. This format also allows restriction of public access to proprietary services, such as continuing medical education (CME) programs for staff, for instance.

A major concern of many healthcare organizations is that of protecting patient, patient care, and financial data. As many organizations continue to seek a universal solution for housing all of their information needs on older mainframe-based systems, a major advantage of creating an intranet is that doing so renders sensitive patient, patient care, and financial data inaccessible to the public. Most of the information that traverses an intranet will not require the same security safeguards required by patient records and financial data. This allows creation of an effective solution for information exchange without the expense of creating costly firewalls or employing other security measures. These two parallel systems each serve to support a specific need and deliver information to the appropriate audience at the appropriate level of security. Financial and patient data are secure from potential public access while the information distributed retains its ease of use.

Intranet Services

Organization-specific information

An intranet represents an opportunity for a healthcare organization to communicate both with its customers and its personnel. A useful analogy in the corporate world is that of an enterprisewide intranet—within whose intranet home computer (known as the intranet host or server) resides the corporation's memory infrastructure. This is where useful information is stored that allows staff to function, either as customers or as employees. The following are some of the benefits of an intranet:

- A patient or doctor's office secretary could use the intranet to produce a map of the organization's campus and print it out to find, say, a specific department (e.g., the laboratory).
- A patient could determine what information is needed by a specific department and download the forms to fill out before visiting that department.
- Physicians and employees, working in an outlying clinic, could easily access a central repository for a schedule of events, presentations, or CME programs and functions.
- Physicians, patients, and employees could learn about their healthcare organization's new capabilities.
- Documents describing the organization's policies could be accessed.

These are but a few examples of how physicians, patients, and employees could usefully query and interact with an intranet. The information can be maintained in a central repository and updated by the responsible departments.

The organization's information section should include a brief synopsis of its history, a description of services offered, and maps related to finding and navigating the hospital campus. Printed materials commonly given to patients presenting for services can be made available electronically. The hospital's mission should be clearly stated, in addition to any specific requirements for admission or treatment. Any information that is deemed either necessary or beneficial to share with the public can be published electronically and made available at the appropriate level of access.

Staff directory

The staff directory will often include a listing of all healthcare providers, their photographs, their curricula vitae, and their special areas of expertise and interest. In some cases, the intranet administrator may permit each practitioner to provide additional information specific to his or her practice. Such information may include maps and location information, pre-visit information for patients, and possibly online registration capabilities to streamline the process of acquiring patient data.

E-mail

An e-mail directory usually includes staff-specific and clinic- or department-specific information in an easy-to-access format, often a web page. Such directories are an excellent way for healthcare organizations to create a sense of community among employees and patients, as well as the general public. From them, electronic mailing lists can be created that distribute e-mail messages to those on the list. In addition, specific announcements can be distributed, e-mail messages can be shared among discussion groups, and staff and patients can engage in an ongoing dialog. E-mailing lists may target groups interested in specific disease topics, individuals involved in fundraising events and activities, professionals interested in specific continuing medical education programs and activities, and so forth.

Image transfer and file transfer protocol site

With the advent of inexpensive methods for digitizing both clinical photographs and radiological images, sharing this type of information as part of an informal or formal consultation has become a reality. The ability to include images in the discussion of a clinical case can be useful in delivering patient care and in providing continuing medical education for the organization's professional staff. Image transfer can be accomplished by digital camera, by direct capture, or by scanning photographs and x-rays. An image can then be transferred as a file to a file transfer protocol site where it can be archived for access at a later time. This site need not be limited to image files; it can also include digitized data files of many types (e.g., software files, data files, document files). Image files can also be sent as file attachments on e-mail messages to other members of the intranet community. As the intranet provides a more secure, private mechanism for direct point-to-point consultation and communication among members of the Intranet community, rather than general discussion of a case, this form of visual communication can be especially advantageous.

Library services

Involving the medical library in the intranet is an integral part of resource sharing. Regional healthcare organizations are often the only facilities within a given referral area with a professionally staffed medical library. Availability of library services on the intranet can increase the use of library services and resources throughout the region. Medical librarians are well aware of the benefits of computer-mediated communication and can be helpful in promoting the concept.

One recent trend in healthcare delivery has been a shift away from the notion that healthcare organizations are illness care centers and toward the idea that, instead, they are as much or more centers of maintaining or promoting health and wellness. Patient education has come to play a key role in effecting this shift. Accordingly, the role of the medical library has also shifted from supporting the medical staff exclusively to supporting and providing resources to patients, as well. A publicly accessible intranet is an excellent means for disseminating such information. Access to the intranet and these library resources can be gained by way of the Internet, organization-based information kiosks, or by terminals hardwired into the intranet at various locations, including medical offices and clinics, throughout the healthcare organization.

Continuing medical education

Conversion of CME presentations to an intranet format is readily accomplished either by use of the organization's internal technical expertise or by outsourcing to vendors specializing in converting traditional presentations (such as noon conferences for the medical staff) into interactive computer-mediated sessions. These sessions can be electronically published, archived, and shared among other institutions networked to the healthcare organization hosting the intranet.

Patient education modules

Patient education is an increasingly important aspect of healthcare delivery. It is also inefficiently accomplished in most clinics, offices, and hospitals. By combining the concepts of computer-based training and information delivery over an intranet, the patient education process is streamlined and can be designed to meet the needs of individual patients. With educational materials available online, patients are given access to these materials either while undergoing treatment at the healthcare organization or at home. By combining readily available patient education materials with custom-designed offerings, each healthcare delivery system is able to design a system to meet its own needs. Software-based patient education materials capable of being distributed over an intranet are relatively easy to create and inexpensive to produce.

Links of professional interest

Organizing the vast array of medically related Internet resources is critical to effective use of these resources by professional members of the organization's intranet community. The task of locating and organizing Internet resources may be assigned to a team of content specialists, who, in effect, serve as agents to healthcare professionals in compiling, organizing, and updating Internet resources that are of special and specialized interest to these professionals. Listings of these resources are then posted to the intranet where they can be readily accessed.

Links of public interest

Links of public interest may be offered as a service not only to members of the organization's intranet community but to members of the larger Internet community, as well. Once connected to the organization's intranet, it makes no difference whether one is seated at a terminal within the organization or at one's home. Public links can be an excellent way of supplementing patient information supplied by other means. Links can be to information created within the organization for specific purposes or to information to be found on the Internet.

Promoting health and wellness, instead of merely treating disease, requires a ready means of educating members of the organization's intranet community and of disseminating information to them efficiently. To these ends, vast numbers of resources are emerging that healthcare organizations can freely use. Organizing the resources and making them easily available to the patients and staff increase the efficiency and efficacy of their use.

Training

One of the more important lessons of the computer revolution is that sufficient training during deployment of new technologies is vital. Healthcare organizations may use their intranets to train members of their intranet communities in its use as well as for general training purposes. For both patients and staff, the organizational intranet is especially well suited to interactive learning, and there are a number of audiovisual and multimedia training modules that are available as interactive teaching tools.

14

The Role of Automation in the Future of Healthcare Delivery

This chapter addresses a variety of automated systems and information technologies that have come into play among healthcare organizations and the networks within which they operate today. Clinical decision support, performance assessment, telemedicine, robotics, and other recent advances in technology within the healthcare field are addressed; an overview of emerging developments that could potentially improve the quality of healthcare in the future is also provided.

Recent advances in automation and information systems technology have combined to slingshot healthcare well into the future. In a relatively short time, the worldwide, computer-driven information revolution has begun to radically alter the way health services are provided. Everything has been affected: from the way the simplest and most mundane of everyday business functions are performed to how complex clinical decisions are made, to how healthcare managers and clinicians communicate. Recent advances in technology have changed even the ways in which clinicians and patients communicate with one another.

In many ways, these changes are driving the formation of integrated delivery systems, and component facilities, to perform in the marketplace. In the future, such changes promise to determine how, when, and where healthcare will be delivered; by whom and to whom; and at what level of intensity, cost, and value. Automation and technology have produced radical changes in how healthcare will be delivered and accessed in the future.

TECHNOLOGIES IMPORTANT TO QUALITY OF CARE

Healthcare quality is ultimately judged by how health services affect a patient's health. The most direct contribution information technology makes toward improving healthcare quality is to provide clinicians with better information about their patients and the health problem at hand. Necessary also are alternative tests and treatments for that particular health problem— preferably when that care is delivered. This chapter discusses the potential for information technologies to improve the healthcare quality.

Some of the most important of these technologies today are:

- the electronic patient record;
- structured data entry;
- advanced human–computer interface technologies;
- portable computers;
- automated capture of data from diagnostic and monitoring equipment;
- relational databases with online query (keyword search and retrieval); and
- knowledge-based computing and computer networks.

Clinical decision support is one approach to improving healthcare and the ways that information technology can enhance clinical decision making. Performance assessment is another approach that involves evaluating health services, providers, and insurance plans. The basic question is whether information technology can improve the accuracy of information needed in clinical decision making, reduce the amount of time necessary to retrieve this information, and make this information accessible at the time and place that care is delivered.

The Electronic Patient Record

One of the best-known technologies for improving patient information is the electronic patient record or, as it is sometimes called, the computerized medical record. This stores patient information taken from a variety of sources, such as the clinic, laboratory, pharmacy, and so forth. As this storage takes place, other technologies for handling patient information may operate in conjunction with the electronic patient record. Overall, these technologies permit faster, easier, and more accurate collection of information about the patient. Clinical examination results are entered by clinicians at or near the time and place that care is delivered, often with the aid of portable computers. Data entry is accomplished by use of such means as onscreen forms and menus with prepared blocks of text that encourage complete data collection. This approach reduces errors, particularly when pen-based computing is used rather than keyboards. Automatic date- and time-stamping of entries can also assist in documenting and tracking patient care and patient care outcomes over time.

Some patient data can be captured directly from diagnostic and moni-toring equipment, bypassing the need for human data entry altogether. Radiographic images, videos, and sound recordings can be digitized, stored, and transmitted electronically. Some patient background information can even be entered into computers by patients themselves. Additionally, in some cases, certain demographic characteristics about the patient can be obtained from other computer databases—such as insurance eligibility files—again avoiding the need for manual data entry.

Using relational databases, information technologies also permit faster, easier, and better search and retrieval information collected about a patient—even while that care is being delivered. Portable computers and advanced human-computer interface technologies are also helpful here. Electronic storage of digitized radiographic images, videos, and sound recordings makes them easier to locate and retrieve. Ever more powerful and flexible graph-ics software and high-resolution displays can also be helpful in organizing and displaying information.

Accessible Online Information on Health and Healthcare

Computer and telecommunications networks, together with online query capability, portable computers, and advanced human–computer interfaces, make information about various health problems more accessible. Many research libraries provide online access to their computerized catalogs and bibliographic databases, which can now be accessed and queried online. Documents can be ordered online from one of the more than 4,000 member libraries of the National Network of Libraries of Medicine.

The National Cancer Institute, a member of that network, maintains the Physician Data Query system, which provides clinicians information via the Internet and by fax regarding various cancers, clinical trials, and indi-viduals and organizations involved in cancer care. The University of Penn-sylvania, meanwhile, maintains a multimedia cancer information resource on the Internet called OncoLink. The Centers for Disease Control provide online access to the full text of their *Morbidity and Mortality Weekly Report* and have also launched *Emerging Infectious Diseases*, an online journal. Any number of biomedical journals are also available online.

Some periodicals, and even complete books and reports, have become available on CD-ROM and can be purchased or obtained through many libraries. Recently released CD-ROM recorders and rewriteable CD-ROM discs now permit updates to their content as knowledge and knowledge bases change. Both CD-ROMs and the Internet permit inclusion of graphics, videos, and sound in text-based documents.

Information technology has also made clinical practice guidelines more accessible. The National Library of Medicine offers online access to practice guidelines developed by several sources, while many private organizations, such as the American Medical Association, have distributed their practice guidelines on CD-ROM and computer diskettes.

Recently, an international movement among researchers and clinicians has developed an approach to clinical problem solving called evidence-based medicine. This involves searching and evaluating research literature to identify findings that can be applied to clinical problems. Evidence-based medicine goes beyond the articles published in clinical journals by its use of careful, systematic literature reviews. Through these reviews, specific information is extracted from each work and compared across texts. The most sophisticated form of such a review has been called *meta-analysis*, which amounts to a synthesis of the results of a number of studies on a given topic. Special journals have been established to summarize and evaluate literature on specific health problems. For instance, the Cochrane Collaboration, an international network of researchers, distributes uncopyrighted results of reviews of randomized controlled trials—or the most reliable evidence from other sources—on selected health problems and posts these to the Internet.

The prospect of making information such as research results available for online query through the Internet has given rise to electronic publishing. Not only are certain peer-reviewed journals available online today, but in some scientific disciplines, such as physics, preliminary results are often distributed over the Internet before they are published.

Computer-based Clinical Decision Support Systems

More and more, sources of clinical decision support are being supplemented by clinical information systems, usually at large teaching hospitals. The simplest of these are library systems or data systems that display information about the patient or the health problem without offering advice. On the other hand, some clinical information systems contain so-called expert systems—knowledge-based systems that can offer clinical decision makers advice about diagnosis, testing, and treatment. The goal of these systems is to provide more complete and more accurate information more quickly to the clinician. In this way, clinical decision making can be improved in terms of patient outcome measures. These systems may also contain other computer applications besides decision support, such as online order-entry that allows the clinician to submit orders for tests and treatments.

Knowledge-based systems designed for clinical use, sometimes called clinical decision support systems, ordinarily involve:

- data on the patient being diagnosed or treated. These are either entered into the system manually, captured automatically from diagnostic or monitoring equipment, or drawn from an electronic patient record;
- a knowledge base that contains rules and decision algorithms that incorporate knowledge and judgment about the health problem at hand and alternative tests and treatments for it. This is mainly in the form of "if-then" statements, such as "if the patient's potassium is less than 3.0 mEq/dl and the patient is on digoxin, then potassium supplementation should be considered"; and
- an "inference engine" that combines information from both the patient data and the knowledge base to perform specified tasks.

Some of the newer clinical decision support systems use probabilistic and adaptive approaches. These may incorporate the use of such technical advances as fuzzy logic, Bayesian networks, or neural networks. Older clinical decision support systems may use simpler deterministic systems, methods, and models, such as decision trees.

Many of the major applications of clinical decision support systems in use today were first implemented 20 to 25 years ago in two pioneer systems:

- the Health Evaluation through Logical Processing (HELP) system developed by Intermountain Health Care and its flagship institution, LDS Hospital, and the University of Utah in Salt Lake City; and
- the Regenstrief Medical Record System (RMRS), developed by the Regenstrief Institute and Indiana University, initially at Wishard Memorial Hospital in Indianapolis.

Components of both of these systems were marketed commercially: HELP by the 3M Company, and RMRS by Shared Medical Systems, Inc., both of which are now among the world's leading information services vendors. Several other clinical decision support systems, or some of their particular applications, are also commercially available.

Computer-based Clinical Protocols

The most advanced clinical decision support systems integrate several applications into the clinical protocols that define a course of treatment. Once again, some are based on deterministic models, while others employ probabi-

listic and adaptive approaches. Converting a clinical protocol into computer-based algorithms involves using clear terminology, examining the logic
of all the linkages among the steps involved in treatment, and—in deterministic models—specifying very exact measures.

Researchers at Intermountain Health Care developed an approach to
quality improvement, called clinical practice improvement, that combined
computer-based clinical protocols, research, and the principles of continuous quality improvement. By using this approach, they were able to develop
protocols for specific health problems based on a review of the literature,
clinician judgment, and analysis of data from an electronic patient record
system. These protocols were refined through discussions among clinicians
and were then used to guide diagnosis and treatment. These protocols were
then further honed and refined against the results of controlled clinical trials.

OTHER POTENTIAL BENEFITS OF INFORMATION TECHNOLOGY

Both clinical protocol development and research can be improved by using
advanced information technologies. Because in today's healthcare organizations most patients receive care from more than one clinician, there are
usually several separate information systems—often one for each department (e.g., inpatient, outpatient, laboratory, and pharmacy). Electronic patient record systems and computer networks within and across healthcare
organizations can aid in tracking all care and patient outcomes. These systems make it easier and more efficient to link the separate records for a
given patient across all departments and caregivers, particularly if a common, unique patient identifier is used. For example, the value of assembling
patient data across several departments was illustrated by research that used
the HELP system at LDS Hospital to identify specific causes of adverse
drug events and hospital-acquired infections. Computer networks across
organizations also permit wider and faster dissemination of treatment protocols and the results of research to remote sites.

An important way for information technologies to enhance the healthcare
quality has been in improving what are known as "outcomes data." These
data are used to determine the effectiveness of health services. Electronic
patient records, structured data entry, advanced human–computer interfaces,
portable computers, and automated data capture from diagnostic and monitoring equipment make the collection of patient data not only faster and
easier but also more complete and accurate. This permits better measurement of patient risk factors, clinical processes, and patient outcomes. Records
or results for patients with a particular health problem—who are treated in

different ways—can be pooled across all clinicians and caregivers, all facilities, and all organizations. In this way, very large databases can be created to assess healthcare effectiveness. Research based on these improved data and data sets has resulted in the creation of the medical knowledge upon which clinical decision support is based.

From the perspective of physicians, one benefit of using information technology in medical practice has become readily apparent: Two malpractice insurance companies began offering reduced premiums to physicians who use specific commercial electronic patient record systems. In many ways, this development reflects the improved patient information and documentation of care that electronic patient records can offer compared with paper-based records.

PERFORMANCE ASSESSMENT

Another approach to improving healthcare quality is called performance assessment, which is an attempt to evaluate and measure the performance of clinicians, caregivers, and health insurance plans by:

- evaluating the performance of clinicians, caregivers, or insurance plans in delivering services to patients;
- giving care providers or insurance plans feedback on their performance to help them improve; and
- giving performance information to payors, purchasers, and consumers to help them select care providers and insurance plans.

Performance measures can focus on several aspects of patient care. Two of the more important of these are:

- the use of services that are considered appropriate for a given health problem; and
- patient outcomes of those services, usually measured by negative outcomes such as deaths, complications, and readmissions.

The kinds of information needed to assess the performance of care providers or insurance plans are much like those needed for clinical decision support. Specifically, such information is likely to include data about individual patients, their health problems, and the types of health services that individual care providers—whether clinicians, facilities, or institutions—use to diagnose, treat, or prevent those problems.

To examine the link between processes and outcomes, performance assessment usually focuses on negative or so-called "adverse" outcomes in such a way as to help identify processes that need correcting. Clinical decision support, on the other hand, focuses on selecting services in advance that are considered to be those the most likely to produce favorable outcomes.

Relationship to Other Recent Trends

The performance assessment approach to quality improvement fits neatly with recent trends toward managed care and toward increasing competition among care providers and insurance plans. Traditional indemnity (e.g., fee-for-service) insurance is seen as creating incentives for providers to over-use health services to maximize income. As this is so, one goal of performance assessment is to reduce unnecessary services to restrain the escalation of healthcare costs.

On the other hand, managed care—which involves payment in advance for healthcare services—is seen as creating incentives for care providers to keep costs lower than the prepayment amount. One way to do this is to reduce the volume and intensity of services that are delivered to patients. If this leads to underuse of services that are necessary to diagnose, treat, or prevent a given health problem, then patients' health status may be negatively affected. Therefore, another goal of performance assessment is to monitor patient outcomes and the rates of use of services that are intended to improve patient outcomes.

The performance assessment approach assumes that, by giving care providers feedback on their performance in terms of patient outcomes, these care providers will be encouraged to improve their processes of care by choosing the most effective services for a specific health problem. Identifying and correcting problems in production processes is one major component of continuous quality improvement in manufacturing—an approach that was later adapted to the healthcare industry. More recently, managed care organizations and even pharmaceutical companies have sought to adapt this continuous improvement approach to manage such costly health problems as diabetes, asthma, and high blood pressure. This approach, known as disease management, involves practice guidelines, outcomes measurement, and feedback to care providers and insurance plans. At the same time, employers and insurance plans have attempted to deal with the rising cost of pharmaceuticals through pharmacy benefit management, which incorporates the principles of disease management with the workings of pharmacy networks, negotiated discounts and rebates, lists of preferred drugs, and online utilization review.

Information Technology and Performance Assessment

Information technology contributes to performance assessment in two ways: first, by improving the measures and data on which those assessments are based and, second, by making the results of assessments, and the measures and data on which they are based, more easily available to payors, purchasers, consumers, and researchers.

By its nature, performance assessment reviews past performance and so cannot employ clinical trials and other forms of forward-looking analysis. Performance assessment thus employs retrospective analysis that involves either data collection or analysis of administrative data, or both. Data are collected mainly through clinician reviews of patient records and surveys of patients and care providers. Administrative data may include hospital discharge abstracts, health insurance claims, or encounter records and enrollment records. Each of these sources has certain limitations that information technology can help overcome.

In sum, advanced information technology—electronic patient records, structured data entry, new human–computer interface technology, portable computers, automated data capture, relational databases with online query, knowledge-based computing, and computer networks—can and does improve the healthcare quality. By enhancing clinical decision support, and by improving data for assessing the health services effectiveness and the performance of healthcare providers and insurance plans, advanced information technology—particularly as exemplified by the electronic medical record—will play an important role in the future of healthcare delivery, the future of healthcare organizations, and the future of the services they provide.

PERFORMANCE INDICATOR PROJECTS (REPORT CARDS)

In recent years, various groups have tried to develop summary sets of performance indicators, commonly called report cards. Such indicators are designed to:

- help consumers, payors, and self-insured purchasers compare and select among providers;
- help consumers and purchasers select among insurance plans; and
- give performance information to accreditation bodies for providers or insurance plans.

Report cards can also be used to provide feedback to providers for quality improvement purposes and to assist public policymakers in regulating plans and formulating health policy. In addition, care providers and insurance plans often use performance indicator projects or favorable results in their marketing efforts. Report cards can also be used to make changes to processes that will improve their scores on performance indicators.

TELEMEDICINE

Telemedicine is defined as the use of information technology to deliver medical services and information from one location to another. Since the

1960s, telecommunication has been used to exchange medical information between sites in both rural and urban areas. One of the earliest applications of telemedicine was at the University of Nebraska where two-way, closed-circuit microwave television was used for psychiatric consultations. Another was in Boston, where a video link was established between a health clinic at Logan Airport and the Massachusetts General Hospital.

Early expansion of telemedicine was affected, however, by the technology's cost and limitations. Recent advances—such as fiber optics, integrated services digital networks, and compressed video—have eliminated or minimized many of these problems. There has lately been a resurgence of private- and public-sector interest in the potential of telemedicine to lower costs, improve quality, and increase access to healthcare, especially for those who live in remote or underserved areas. The technology is not only better; it has become much less expensive.

Although telemedicine has been practiced for more than 35 years, it is still in its early stages of development. Once it comes into its own, however, it promises to have a greater impact on the future of medicine than any other technology to date. In the final analysis, telemedicine will bring enhanced access to medical care and create a global healthcare network. Realizing this, organizations like the World Health Organization and the European Commission are exploring its potential.

Telemedicine's Potential Effects

Parts of the United States that are sparsely populated have difficulty attracting and retaining health professionals, as well as supporting local hospitals and clinics. There are a number of reasons that isolated areas have difficulty attracting and retaining healthcare professionals, including:

- Medical practice is often more demanding and less lucrative than in larger centers.
- Care providers may feel isolated from mentors, colleagues, and the information resources necessary to support them personally and professionally.
- Equipment may be less up-to-date and facilities less than adequate.

Interestingly, similar problems often plague the healthcare delivery to large inner-city populations. Telemedicine is a tool that can help address problems of care-provider distribution by improving communication capabilities and by providing convenient access to up-to-date information, consultations, and other forms of support.

Using telecommunications to deliver health services can reduce costs, improve quality, and improve access to care to medically underserved areas of the country. Although the extent of this potential can only be guessed at this time, if research results prove positive, telemedicine is likely to become a fairly routine use of information technology over the next five to ten years. One thing is certain—no single technological solution will work for all healthcare organizations and for all communities. Every setting is unique, and systems designed to address access problems must be tailored to meet the particular needs and culture of each facility and each community, whether the setting is rural or urban.

Even so, it may be a number of years before telemedicine is used widely enough to be properly evaluated for its effectiveness and efficiency. As with all new technologies, however, there will be effects that cannot be anticipated. As studies are needed to determine telemedicine's potential benefits, such research has just begun to take place. With Congress, the Clinton administration, the healthcare industry, and consumers all searching for ways to reduce the costs of delivering healthcare, the potential of telemedicine has begun to be carefully scrutinized.

Part V

The Future of the U.S. Healthcare System

15

Toward a Broader View of Healthcare

Stuart A. Wesbury, Jr.*

Even though no clear picture of our nation's future healthcare system exists, the number of proposals trying to describe it is too great to be counted. These proposals have come from congressional committees and from a variety of governmental agencies, healthcare associations, and professional societies, as well as from many public and private bodies. The only commonality among these proposals is that they call for change. Given the extent of pressure and concern, future change is inevitable. This we must expect.

A brief look backward is necessary if we are to understand the problems we face today—let alone predict the future and anticipate change. An interesting way of examining the past and the changes that have occurred is to divide the twentieth century into healthcare eras or periods. From an overall perspective, I believe the following present a useful description of such eras:

- 1900–1945, the era of public health
- 1945–1970s, the era of technology and increased access
- 1970s–1990s, the era of cost containment and organizational change.

---

* Stuart A. Wesbury, Jr., Ph.D., has been a pharmacist, hospital administrator, university professor, healthcare consultant, and president and chief executive officer of the American College of Healthcare Executives. He is currently Research Professor, School of Health Administration and Policy, Arizona State University, Tempe, Arizona.

THE ERA OF PUBLIC HEALTH (1900–1945)

During this era, the healthcare system was heavily influenced by public health issues. This was a time of significant investment in infrastructure (i.e., water systems, sewer systems, sanitation, communicable disease prevention efforts, etc.). Although the beginnings of the modern-day hospital were in place, hospitals emphasized care, not cure. Anesthesia was still in its infancy, and surgical and other specialties in medicine were just beginning to emerge. Despite the lack of technology, American citizens began to enjoy increasing longevity and better health overall. However, much of this progress—if not most of it—was the result of the effectiveness of the public health portion of our health system. Modern medicine was not yet on the scene.

TECHNOLOGY AND INCREASED ACCESS (1945–1970s)

The end of World War II created a new era. The outlook now was heavily influenced by an explosion of interest in science and a corresponding expansion of the national investment in healthcare. The scientific neorenaissance brought with it exciting new technology and new ways of diagnosing and treating a wide variety of diseases and illnesses. Sophisticated surgical techniques were instituted and gained widespread credibility as a large number of new medical specialties evolved. Connected with these scientific advances was the creation of new professions and roles within the healthcare system. Job descriptions in medical technology, radiological technology, and similar fields were changing almost daily, and new professional categories were being created to go along with emerging technology. Titles used commonly today, such as profusion technician, cardiovascular technician, and respiratory therapist, had their start at this time. Suddenly, we were treating diseases previously almost unknown, and we began to think that every disease could be conquered.

A parallel development during this era of technology and increased access was the desire to make healthcare available to all. In the 1940s, the Hill–Burton hospital construction program was created, leading to the construction of hundreds of hospitals in small towns across the United States along with significant expansions and improvements of hospitals in larger cities. Great concern was raised about healthcare for the poor, and programs to provide the poor with access to care were initiated. The most significant development in this regard was the creation of Medicare and Medicaid in the mid-1960s. Whether by definitive policy or by accident, the United States was moving aggressively toward making high-quality, high-cost care available to all citizens. This was indeed an exciting era.

COST CONTAINMENT AND ORGANIZATIONAL CHANGE (1970s–1990s)

As might be expected in retrospect, the significant expansions of the technology and access era had to come to an end. The pressures on the federal government and on business to sustain those increases in cost necessary to provide for this dramatic expansion of health services resulted in active debates. Many raised concerns about our ability to continue this rapid expansion of healthcare services. One result of the uneasiness was interest in investigating alternative systems of healthcare delivery to save money. The HMO became a popular example of what might be done to slow healthcare cost increases. Concerns were raised about possible unnecessary uses of hospitals and other healthcare services. Companies began to ask questions about the cost of health plan fringe benefits for their employees.

This change of focus was not all negative: We *did* discover that healthcare services could be made available and possibly less costly under a variety of alternative delivery systems. As already mentioned, the HMO was popularized along with the preferred provider organization and other so-called managed care alternatives.

On the national front, Medicare made a dramatic change in its method of paying hospitals. Instead of making payments on the basis of the cost of providing services, the federal Medicare program adopted a prospective payment system, which paid the hospital on the basis of the diagnosis of the patient's particular problem. Thus, a specific price was set for each of 467 diagnosis-related groups representing the gamut of diagnoses that might require a patient's hospitalization. For example, a specific predetermined price for an appendectomy for a patient on Medicare was established. That price was paid to the hospital regardless of the length of time the patient stayed in the hospital or the number of services provided. This dramatic change greatly influenced the patient's length of stay and led to shortened average lengths of stay for almost every diagnostic category. Further, we saw the continued development of new technology that allowed more and more procedures to be performed in an outpatient setting. Hospitals found themselves making major changes in their organizational structure to accommodate these shifts toward more outpatient services. In fact, some healthcare experts anticipate that 50 percent or more of a hospital's income will come, in the not-too-distant future, from outpatient services.

Despite the major changes brought about during this era of cost containment and organizational change, the healthcare system continues to suffer from the problem of increasing costs. Today, the government is searching steadily for ways to lessen the burden of health services costs to its citizens, and virtually all of the nation's industries and businesses, as we know, consider healthcare costs to be excessive. At the same time, in 1999, the number of the medically uninsured was estimated to be about 43 million, with many other additional millions significantly underinsured.

Further, when levels of improvement in longevity, quality of life, and overall health are considered, it appears that the nation still has significant problems despite the rapid growth of the healthcare system. Comparative statistics examining longevity and rates of infant death raise serious questions about our health services system's efficacy. Why, if we spend so much, are we not living longer than people who live in other developed nations? Why don't more babies survive birth or their first year of life? Are we really getting the best value for our healthcare dollar? Why can't we do better? Interestingly, answers to these questions can shed some light on the description of health services in the future.

The fundamental question is this: Why, with all this new technology and all of these additional dollars spent for health services, do we not have better national health? This is a straightforward question that deserves an answer.

In 1972, Mark Lalonde, minister of National Health and Welfare for Canada, issued a report entitled "A New Perspective on the Health of Canadians," which clearly stated that the Canadian healthcare system and all of its hospitals, clinics, physicians, nurses, other professionals, and technologies was not the most important factor in determining the health of the Canadian people. More important were the health consequences of human biology, including heredity; the environment; and the individual's lifestyle. Clearly and unequivocally, Mr. Lalonde underscored the marginal effect on health that a healthcare system provides. The lesson learned from this report is the straightforward conclusion that if we want to improve health, we should begin to pay more attention to factors other than the healthcare system. It would appear that neither Canada nor the United States has learned this lesson. In both countries, little attention is paid to the factors of human biology, environment, and lifestyle. While Canada has done a better job than the United States in holding its health services costs down, it has not done so through investing in these other factors. In both countries, untold numbers of dollars are spent on services and treatments to help people fight diseases rather than on attempts to prevent diseases from occurring in the first place. For example, little connection has been made in either country with regard to the effects of education and nutrition on healthcare. This is despite our clear knowledge that many diseases and conditions can be prevented when people have appropriate knowledge of what constitutes healthy behaviors and develop good nutritional habits.

In summary, our nation's healthcare system has had an interesting evolution. We have moved, in the twentieth century, from a system heavily oriented toward public health to one heavily oriented toward high technology. We have moved from our position as a nation willing to invest growing sums of money in the health of its people to a nation now questioning what it is already spending—let alone whether it is interested—in providing more money in the future. Our health services data now indicate that improvements of overall health and longevity are no longer occurring at the rates they once did. In fact, for some segments of our population (e.g., African-American males), health statistics indicate a deterioration in the quality and length of life. But we have also begun to see more clearly that health is a function of many things, not just of the availability of healthcare services. Therefore, as we begin to prepare for the future, we must begin to find ways to improve the return on our investment in healthcare and to broaden our perspective on those varied elements leading to improved health.

FUTURE DIRECTIONS

While some directions for the future are fairly clear, much of what is to come is virtually unpredictable. Our biggest problem in trying to identify the nature of future change lies in our inability to judge the roles that major healthcare forces will play. These forces include the federal government, state governments, major employers, national associations of employers, and the associations and professional societies representing the healthcare system. While each of these groups has an important role to play with respect to health services developments, significant confusion appears to exist within each of them regarding where the healthcare system should be going. For example, despite the circulation of numerous major committee and task force reports, the federal government remains years away from developing a coherent national health policy or program. The same can be said for our nation's employers. Many companies claim to have major problems with their healthcare expenses, while other companies consider their healthcare expenses not serious enough to require significant attention. The uninsured and underinsured populations lack sufficient political clout to force governments to deal with their problems effectively. Thus, the major question is: When, if ever, will the collective concerns of these major groups reach a point of concern sufficient to force major national decisions? Today, nothing is happening to provide an answer to this question. We are still far from creating a national focus on a rational reorganization of our healthcare system.

Although we cannot predict the initiation of a broad national focus on healthcare reform, some more narrow predictions can be made with a high level of certainty.

1. **Technology will continue to provide exciting breakthroughs in the diagnosis and treatment of disease.** Much emphasis in technological development will be placed on the development of noninvasive procedures as we continue to build upon major imaging innovations. Many other important introductions will take place through developments in miniaturization and in the use of lasers. Surgical procedures will therefore be simplified, with some major procedures totally disappearing. Continued progress will be made, of course, in the discovery and development of new drugs and in our ability to adapt technological developments that occur elsewhere (e.g., in space exploration, genetics, and so on).

2. **Inpatient hospitalization will continue to play a very important but continually smaller role.** The major movement toward out patient versus inpatient care that started in the 1980s will continue into the twenty-first century. Technological developments will fuel this move, along with pressures from cost-containment interests. Thus, hospitals will be required to adjust to these movements continuously as fewer patients seek inpatient services and as those who do will tend to be more seriously ill, on average, than persons now receiving inpatient care.

3. **Our aging population will continue to add pressures to our healthcare system.** The acute care and long-term needs of the elderly population are not well-understood. More attention will be focused on understanding the complex acute and chronic conditions that affect the elderly. The health problems of the elderly often interact with multiple elements of their everyday life. Healthcare professionals are often unprepared to deal with such interactions. We must become more skilled in helping the elderly maintain good health and reach and maintain a better quality of life. An important side issue is the growing political impact of issues surrounding our senior citizens, who are a major voting block and have significant political influence.

4. **Health services costs will continue to grow at rates greater than inflation.** This means that healthcare costs will never leave the nation's list of problems. Cost, coupled with a focus on the uninsured or underinsured, will also be an issue in healthcare and in the political forum.

5. **Despite progress in treating patients with HIV/AIDS, the future extent of the problem of caring for those with HIV/AIDS is still not clear.** Will a cure for AIDS be found? Will educational programs intended to prevent AIDS be successful? No real answer to these questions can currently be offered. AIDS will be a continuing problem to the healthcare system.

6. **Medical ethics, including issues such as rationing, the right to die, and organ allocation, will plague our healthcare system.** Easy answers will not be forthcoming, and the political system and the public at large will be deeply involved in ethical issues.

7. **The quality and outcomes of care will receive greater attention.** Not only does concern for quality and outcome assessment relate to the desire to provide proper patient care, but a better understanding of quality and outcomes also will allow us to effectively compare various approaches to dealing with specific problems. In other words, developments in the quality of care and assessment of outcomes will help us make better—and less costly—decisions about healthcare delivery.

8. **Managed care has become a target for many who are reacting to stories about patients who have been denied care.** Concern over cost containment is forcing many to look more critically at managed care. Are patients being denied medical care? Is this widespread? Are government regulations sufficient to ensure that quality care is delivered by managed care organizations? This issue will continue to receive much attention both from the political and media perspectives.

9. **In the last ten years, the healthcare delivery system has undergone extensive change.** A key outcome has been fewer but larger organizations. Numerous multihospital systems have been created. Integrated healthcare delivery systems have become the vogue. "Large is better" seems to be the underlying driving force. While such systems seem logical reactions to marketplace challenges and opportunities (e.g., economies of scale, broad-based marketing, and provision of full-service healthcare), we are still learning how they can be managed. It is already clear that the structure of the healthcare delivery system will continue to change. The learning process will continue, and experimentation with new delivery systems will provide many opportunities for creativity.

This list of predictions clearly indicates that our role as managers in healthcare can only get more complex. All of us will be responsible for understanding issues that go far beyond our disciplinary areas. Whether you are managing a laboratory, a business office, the operating room, or an outpatient clinic, you will need to understand the total health services environment and the point at which the work you do fits into the broader picture. Narrow minds and a narrow focus among our healthcare managers will lead to inappropriate and uneconomical decisions. Collectively, we all face similar problems, and we can benefit greatly from mutual interaction.

One other development must be discussed as we look toward the future—the growing acceptance of health as a "community affair." This concept should not be taken lightly. The implication is that, despite actions taken or not taken at the federal and state levels, each community must accept substantial responsibility for the care of its own citizens. The community is where the greatest creativity and innovation can evolve.

Not too many years ago, it was predicted that the United States would see the creation of perhaps no more than ten "supermeds," organizations created to integrate the delivery of health services over large regional areas covering many states. For some, this was felt to be the panacea— a way to control healthcare costs and assure overall healthcare effectiveness. We know now that this represents an impossible alternative. A few regional systems cannot effectively coordinate care at the local level. Each community has its own mix of health services providers and its own healthcare-related problems. Real problem solving must begin within the community.

Recognizing this fact has created some exciting ventures in many of the nation's communities. Healthcare leaders, business leaders, community leaders, and political leaders have joined forces to view more broadly their local community health problems. Community hospitals and other healthcare organizations have created a wide variety of programs supporting healthy lifestyles and illness prevention. Many communities have created forums for discussing health issues, including issues of medical ethics. Open community discussions can help foster an understanding of healthcare problems and ways in which a community might respond to complex and sensitive issues. Further, in communities where an openness exists in discussing healthcare issues, new approaches to healthcare delivery have a higher chance of adoption and success. The community is where the health action is. Until more direction is forthcoming from the national or state level, it is clear that the change, if any, will be created at the community level.

As stated earlier, many unknowns still exist with respect to the future. When will the cost of healthcare get so high that government and business together decide to take a stand and create a national health policy? Another important question is whether enough of us will ever accept that the quality of life and the quality of our nation's health are far more directly linked to factors not related to health services delivery. Finally, can we count on people to do something about their own lifestyles and to develop greater concerns about the environment and other controllable particulars that contribute directly to our well-being? These philosophical questions are critical and will force us to keep a broader perspective in mind. The authors of the fifth— perhaps even sixth—edition of this book will still be wrestling with some of the same dilemmas if we cannot accept the fact that health services themselves contribute little to our overall health and the quality of our lives. We must act with the knowledge that many other factors have a great impact on our nation's health. We must think more broadly. May we all carry this message throughout our professional careers.

Appendix:

Professional Healthcare Associations

AMERICAN COLLEGE OF HEALTHCARE EXECUTIVES

One North Franklin Street, Suite 1700
Chicago, IL 60606-3491

Historical Background

The American College of Hospital Administrators was founded in 1933 by 18 administrators and 2 hospital magazine editors who met, on invitation, "to create a profession devoted to improving care for patients through scientific hospital administration" *(A Venture Forward)*. It was renamed in 1985 as the American College of Healthcare Executives (ACHE) as the field expanded to include many more types of healthcare organizations and management.

ACHE is an international professional society of nearly 30,000 healthcare executives. The College is known for its prestigious credentialing and educational programs, and its annual Congress on Healthcare Management, which draws more than 4,000 participants each year. ACHE is also known for its journal, *Journal of Healthcare Management,* and magazine, *Healthcare Executive*, as well as ground-breaking research and career development and public policy programs. ACHE's publishing division, Health Administration Press, is one of the largest publishers of books and journals on all aspects of health services management in addition to textbooks for use in college and university courses. Through such efforts, ACHE works toward its goal of improving the healthcare status of society by advancing healthcare management excellence.

Objectives

1. To establish standards of competence, to promote excellence in healthcare management, and to formulate and maintain a code of ethics for the profession;
2. To elevate the standards of efficiency and effectiveness of healthcare management;
3. To develop and promote standards of education and training for healthcare executives;
4. To provide a method for conferring the status of Fellow and to recognize individuals who have performed or have provided noteworthy service in the field of healthcare management;
5. To educate the public, healthcare professionals, and members of governing bodies of healthcare organizations to understand the issues surrounding the practice of healthcare management, including the special role of education and experience;
6. To provide for healthcare executives the opportunity for gaining continuing education, peer recognition, and expanded development in the profession; and
7. To represent the professional interest of healthcare executives in the development and implementation of public policy in concert with appropriate organizations.

Scope of Activities

1. *Liaison:* The College represents the healthcare management profession at the national level and maintains formal liaisons with many organizations in healthcare-related fields.
2. *Membership:* The College, through an extensive program for advancement, grants recognition to those affiliates achieving a standard of excellence within the profession. Membership categories are Member, Diplomate, Fellow, Honorary Fellow, Faculty Associate, Candidate for Member, International Associate, Life Diplomate, Life Fellow, and Retired Member. A category, Honorary Fellow, is granted to distinguished men and women who have made an exceptional contribution to the field.
3. *Education:* The College conducts a comprehensive program of continuing education for its affiliates.
4. *Research:* The College's broad research program expands the body of knowledge available to healthcare management and provides increased support for healthcare executives.

5. *Publications:* Health Administration Press, a division of the College's Foundation, publishes a number of books each year as well as several journals. Journals include the *Journal of Healthcare Management, Frontiers of Health Services Management*, and *HSR: Health Services Research* .

6. *Communications:* The College's Division of Communications provides affiliates with ACHE-related information with the *Annual Report & Reference Guide*, links them to one another through the Member Directory, and informs them of trends, issues, and developments in the healthcare field through the bimonthly *Healthcare Executive*, ACHE's official magazine.

Total membership: 28,418

Sources: American College of Healthcare Executives. 1999. Description of ACHE; ACHE Fact Sheet [Online information. Retrieved 4/22/99]. http://www.ache.org

American College of Healthcare Executives. 1998. *Annual Report and Reference Guide.* Chicago: ACHE, Department of Communications.

AMERICAN HOSPITAL ASSOCIATION

One North Franklin Street
Chicago, IL 60606

Historical Background

In 1899, eight hospital superintendents gathered in Cleveland, Ohio, to exchange ideas, compare methods of management, and discuss hospital economics and other subjects of common interest. The original group called itself the Association of Hospital Superintendents. In 1906, with membership at 234, the association adopted a new constitution and bylaws and renamed itself the American Hospital Association (AHA).

The mission of AHA is to advance the health of individuals and communities. AHA leads, represents and serves health care provider organizations that are accountable to the community and committed to health improvement.

Scope of Activities

Through representation and advocacy activities, AHA ensures that members' perspectives and needs are heard and addressed in national health policy development, legislative and regulatory debates, and judicial matters. Advocacy efforts include lobbying the legislative and executive branches and include the legislative and regulatory arenas. Complementing the national health care agenda for health delivery restructuring are resources to help executive leadership implement change at the community level, including:

- Customized membership services that help hospitals and other health care providers form integrated networks for patient care
- Research and demonstration projects on innovations in the structuring and delivery of health care services
- Educational programs and opportunities
- Data gathering and information analysis to support policy and development and track trends in hospitals and health care services
- Communications and publications to keep members informed of national developments and trends and their impact on local communities
- Professional developments for health care managers in personal membership groups

Total membership: 5,000 hospitals and healthcare institutions, 600 associate member organizations, and 40,000 individuals active in the healthcare field.

Source: American Hospital Association. 1999. History of the AHA; About AHA [Online information. Retrieved 4/22/99]. http://www.aha.org/about/history.html

AMERICAN MEDICAL ASSOCIATION

515 North State Street
Chicago, IL 60610

Mission

Founded in 1847, the American Medical Association (AMA) is a voluntary service organization of physicians, from every segment of medicine, whose mission is to promote the science and art of medicine and betterment of public health.

Health Interests

1. The AMA represents a large portion of the nation's physicians and medical students. It does so through its House of Delegates, the national policymaking body of the medical profession, whose members come from federal service groups and from the AMA's federation of local and national, medical, and specialty societies.
2. Councils of the AMA, composed of physicians who are experts in relevant fields, strive to upgrade public health and ensure high standards of medical trust, education, and care.
3. The AMA is the world's largest publisher of scientific and medical information. Published in eleven languages and distributed throughout the world, the *Journal of the American Medical Association* (*JAMA*) is the world's most widely read medical journal. The AMA also publishes ten monthly medical specialty journals. Social and economic health news is covered weekly in the award-winning *American Medical News*. Every member of the AMA receives *JAMA* and *American Medical News* each week.
4. The AMA houses one of the nation's largest medical libraries, with more than 25,000 books and subscriptions to 1,500 journals in medicine and allied sciences.
5. The AMA has access to worldwide information through more than 150 computer databases covering the biological, physical, and social sciences, as well as clinical medicine and healthcare administration. AMA's *Physician Masterfile* maintains data on all U.S. physicians and medical students, including nonmembers.
6. The AMA and the Association of American Medical Colleges jointly sponsor the liaison committee, which accredits MD programs in all U.S. and Canadian medical schools.

Total membership: 297,000 physicians

Source: American Medical Association

AMERICAN NURSES ASSOCIATION

600 Maryland Avenue, SW
Suite 100 West
Washington, DC 20024-2571

Historical Background

The American Nurses Association (ANA) was founded in 1896 as the Nurse Associated Alumnae of the United States and Canada, an organization that became the American Nurses Association in 1911. ANA is a full-service professional organization representing the nation's entire registered nurse population.

Long-Term Mission

The ANA's mission is to improve health standards and the availability of health care services for all people, foster high standards for nursing, stimulate and promote the professional development of nurses, and advance their economic and general welfare.

Short-Term Vision

The ANA strives to assure quality health care for all by protecting and enhancing professional nursing practice in all environments.

Objectives

1. To foster high standards of nursing practice
2. To promote the economic and general welfare of nurses in the workplace
3. To project a positive and realistic view of nursing
4. To lobby the Congress and regulatory agencies on health care issues affecting nurses and the public.

Scope of Activities

1. *Nursing practice:* The professional association establishes the standards of professional practice, promotes adherence to ethical standards through a Code for Nurses, and advises on legal aspects of practice.
2. *Nursing education:* The ANA works to set standards and policies for nursing education. It holds national annual meetings and educational conferences.
3. *Nursing services:* The ANA works to improve the quality of nursing and patient services in all settings.

4. *Publications:* The ANA publishes *The American Nurse*, the official publication of the ANA. American Nurses Publishing, the publishing program of the American Nurses Foundation, publishes books and visuals on a variety of cutting-edge programs and nursing and healthcare issues.

5. *General activities:* Other activities include active involvement in economic and general welfare, government relations, intergroup relations, international relations, professional credentials, public relations, and research and statistics. The ANA is a federation of 53 constituent associations (all 50 states plus the District of Columbia, Guam, and the Virgin Islands).

Total membership: over 180,000

Source: American Nurses Association. 1999. ANA at Work [Online information. Retrieved 4/22/99]. http://www.ana.org/ or http://www.nursingworld.org/about/index.htm

AMERICAN PUBLIC HEALTH ASSOCIATION

800 I St., NW
Washington, DC 20001-3710

Historical Background

The American Public Health Association (APHA) was founded in 1872 as a result of the public health movement's efforts to combat yellow fever and other diseases. Since then, APHA and its members have contributed to many of the most extraordinary social and health achievements of modern times—achievements that have increased average life expectancy from 45 to more than 75 years. It is the oldest and largest association of public health professionals in the world.

Objectives

APHA seeks to improve the public's health, promote the scientific and professional foundation of public health practice and policy, advocate the conditions for healthy society, emphasize prevention, and enhance the ability of members to promote and protect environmental and community health.

Scope of Activities

APHA brings together researchers, health service providers, administrators, teachers, and other health care workers in a unique, multidisciplinary environment of professional exchange, study, and action. The association works on many fronts to advance health priorities, including public health and managed care, children's health, public health infrastructure and the environments relating to health. APHA houses the Secretariat of the World Federation of Public Health Associations, which brings together health leaders from 55 countries. APHA holds an annual meeting, which is the largest forum in the world for professional dialogue on public health and hosts nearly 1,000 scientific sessions. On a monthly basis, the association publishes the *American Journal of Public Health* and *The Nation's Health* newspaper, the highest-circulated periodical in the field. APHA is also the foremost publisher of periodicals on public health topics, with more than 50 titles.

Total membership: over 32,000 individual members, with an additional 20,000 state and local affiliate members

Source: American Public Health Association. 1999. About APHA; APHA Membership Information [Online information. Retrieved 4/22/99]. http://www.apha.org/membership/basic.htm/

JOINT COMMISSION ON ACCREDITATION OF HEALTHCARE ORGANIZATIONS

One Renaissance Boulevard
Oakbrook Terrace, IL 60181

An independent, not-for-profit organization, the Joint Commission on Accreditation of Healthcare Organizations (JCAHO) is the nation's oldest and largest standards-setting and accrediting body in health care. Currently, the Joint Commission evaluates and accredits more than 18,000 health care organizations and programs in the United States, including almost 11,000 hospitals and home health care organizations, as well as over 7,000 other health care organizations that provide long-term care, behavioral health care, laboratory, and ambulatory care services. The Joint Commission also accredits health plans, integrated delivery networks, and other managed care entities.

Accreditation is recognized nationwide as a symbol of quality indicating that an organization meets certain performance standards. To earn and maintain accreditation, an organization must undergo an onsite survey by a Joint Commission survey team at least every three years. The Joint Commission's standards address the organization's level of performance in key functional areas, such as patient rights, and the standards focus not simply on what the organization *has* but what it actually *does*. Standards set forth performance expectations for activities that affect the quality of patient care—if an organization does the right things and does them well, there is a strong likelihood that its patients will experience good outcomes. The Joint Commission develops its standards in consultation with health care experts, providers, measurement experts, purchasers, and consumers.

In 1997, the Joint Commission introduced ORYX: The Next Evolution in Accreditation, an initiative to integrate performance measurement into the accreditation process. The long-range goal of the ORYX initiative is to establish a data-driven, continuous survey and accreditation process to complement the standards-based assessment.

The Joint Commission sponsors a variety of education programs and provides relevant publications for healthcare professionals. It is committed to offering standards-related educational support for the organizations it accredits and to advancing provider understanding of current concepts, performance measurement, and improvement.

The Joint Commission provides a comprehensive guide on the Internet designed to help individuals learn more about the quality of healthcare organizations. Quality Check™, located on the Joint Commission's website at www.jcaho.org, lists of the more than 18,000 Joint Commission–accredited health care organizations and programs throughout the United States. In addition, the Joint Commission offers to the public performance reports that provide useful and understandable information about the performance of all organizations accredited by the Joint Commission.

Source: Joint Commission on Accreditation of Healthcare Organizations. 1999. [Online information. Retrieved 4/21/99] http://www.jcaho.org

Suggested Readings

ADMITTING

Abernathy, C.A., and J.E. Ramsey. 1997. "The Hospital Evolution To Discharge Planning Automation." *NAHAM Management Journal* 24(1): 3–5.

Clerkin, D., P.J. Fos, and F.E. Petry. 1995. "A Decision Support System for Hospital Bed Assignment." *Hospital & Health Services Administration* 40(3): 386–400.

Dougherty, R. 1993. "Resource Scheduling: Improving Services Through Access Management." *NAHAM Management Journal* 20(1): 12–13.

Hutchins, J. 1991. "Satellite Registration Program: A Decentralized System to Meet Customer Needs." *NAHAM Management Journal* 16(4): 22–23.

Nickelson, D.E. 1997. "Coming Changes to the Hospital Admitting Environment." *NAHAM Management Journal* 23(4): 21.

Somers, M. 1994. "Enhancing Customer Service in the Admitting Process." *Healthcare Financial Management* 48(9): 68, 70.

ENVIRONMENTAL SERVICES

Phillips, H.P. 1998. "Promoting Professionalism." *Executive Housekeeping Today* 19(1): 4–6.

James, R.B. 1996. "Quality and Efficiency Are No Accident." *Executive Housekeeping Today* 17(12): 8–9.

Janiak, A.C. 1993. "Executive Sets High Standards for Caring and Compassion." *Executive Housekeeping Today* 14(10): 4–5.

Marinik, L.M. 1996. "Delivering Tender Loving Care: A Way Of Life." *Executive Housekeeping Today* 17(7): 4–6.

FINANCIAL SERVICES

Clement, J.P., and D.J. Hansen. 1994. "Health Care Financial Management Curriculum: Views of Practitioners and Academics." *Journal of Health Administration Education* 12(1): 39–45.

Jones, S.B. 1995. "Quality Improvement in Hospitals: How Much Does it Reduce Healthcare Costs?" *Journal of Healthcare Quality* 17(5): 11–13, Quiz 13, 48.

FOOD AND NUTRITIONAL SERVICES

Biesemeier, C., and C.S. Chima. 1997. "Computerized Patient Record: Are We Prepared for our Future Practice?" *Journal of the American Dietetics Association* 97(10): 1099–1104.

Laramee, S.H. 1996. "Nutritional Services In Managed Care: New Paradigms for Dietitians." *Journal of the American Dietetics Association* 96(4): 335–336.

Stahl, P., and M.B. Andrews. 1996. "Vertical Integration is Changing the Landscape of the Health Care System: New Opportunities for Dietetics Professionals." *Journal of the American Dietetics Association* 96(12): 12–40.

HEALTHCARE ORGANIZATION LEADERSHIP— VISION, MISSION, STRATEGY, AND IMPLEMENTATION

American College of Healthcare Executives. 1998. "Professional Policy Statement: Board Certification in Healthcare Management, November 1997." *Healthcare Executive* 13(1): 55.

Bartling, A.C. 1997. "Governance Challenges For Managed Care Organizations." *Healthcare Executive* 11(5): 18–21.

Clement, D.G., and T.T. Wan. 1997. "Mastering Health Care Executive Education: Creating Transformational Competence." *Journal of Health Administration Education* 15(4): 265–274.

Davis, E. 1997. "The Leadership Role of Health Services Managers." *International Journal of Health Care Quality Assurance* 10(4–5): i–iv.

Manion, J. 1998. *From Management to Leadership*. Chicago: American Hospital Association Publication.

Maun, C. 1997. "Are You in Charge? Being a Leader is More than Having a Title." *Balance* 1(3): 20–1, 37.

Reinertsen, J.L. 1995. "The New Knowledge Needed for Health Care Administrators." *Journal of Health Administration Education* 13(1): 39–51.

Scavotto, M. 1994. "The New Trustee." *Health Progress* 75(4): 46–51.

Umiker, W. 1998. "From Technical Professional to Group Leader." *Health Care Supervisor* 16(3): 1–8.

THE GOVERNING BOARD—TRUSTEE LEADERSHIP

Campbell, S. 1998. "The Future of Hospital and Health System Governing Boards." *Health Care Strategic Management* 16(3): 18–19.

Conger, J.A., D. Finegold, and E.E. Lawler. 1998. "Appraising Boardroom Performance." *Harvard Business Review* 76(1): 136–48.

Dolan, T.C. 1994. "Hospital Leadership Team: Roles and Responsibilities." *Trustee* 47(1): 16–7.

Pointer, D.D., and C.W. Ewell. 1995. "Really Governing: What Type of Work Should Boards Be Doing?" *Hospital & Health Services Administration* 40(3): 315–31.

SERVICE VOLUNTEERS AND COMMUNITY SUPPORT

Hospitals and Health Networks. 1997. "Health Care Organizations Value their Volunteers." 71(7): 16–7.

MEDICAL STAFF LEADERSHIP

Bluestein, P. 1995. "Physicians in Transition." *Physician Executive* 21(12): 16–24.

Curry, W. 1994. *The Physician Executive: New Leadership in Health Care Management*. Tampa, FL: American College of Physician Executives.

Olson, D.A. 1997. "And a Doctor Shall Lead Them." *Health Systems Review* 30(5): 33–5, 48–9.

Stone, D.A. 1997. "The Doctor as Businessman: The Changing Politics of a Culture." *Journal of Healthcare Politics* 22(2): 533–56.

HEALTHCARE ADMINISTRATIVE LEADERSHIP

American College of Healthcare Executives. "Professional Policy Statement: Board Certification in Healthcare Management, November 1997." *Healthcare Executive* 13(1): 55.

Clement, D.G., and T.T. Wan. 1997. "Mastering Health Care Executive Education: Creating Transformational Competence." *Journal of Health Administration Education* 15(4): 265–74.

Reinertsen, J.L. 1995. "The New Knowledge Needed for Health Care Administrators." *Journal of Health Administration Education* 13(1): 39–51.

Umiker, W. 1998. "From Technical Professional to Group Leader." *Health Care Supervisor* 16(3): 1–8.

MANAGEMENT OF HEALTHCARE ORGANIZATIONS/ INTEGRATED DELIVERY SYSTEMS/MANAGED CARE

Brown, M. 1995. *Integrated Health Care Delivery.* Gaithersburg, MD: Aspen Publishers.

Carson, K., P. Carson, and C.W. Roe. 1995. *Management of Healthcare Organizations.* Cincinnati, OH: South-Western College Publishing.

Coile, R. 1997. *Millennium Management.* Chicago: Health Administration Press.

Conrad, D. 1997. *Integrated Delivery Systems.* Chicago: Health Administration Press.

Griffith, J. 1998. *Designing 21st Century Healthcare.* Chicago: Health Administration Press.

Kongstvedt, P. 1995. *Essentials of Managed Care.* Gaithersburg, MD: Aspen Publishers.

Lerner, W. 1997. *Anatomy of a Merger.* Chicago: Health Administration Press.

Porter, R. 1998. *The Greatest Benefit to Mankind.* New York: W.W.Norton and Company.

Rakich, J., B. Longest, and K. Darr. 1992. *Managing Health Services Organizations,* 3rd Ed. Baltimore, MD: Health Professions Press.

Shortell, S., R. Gillies, D. Anderson, K. Erickson, and J. Mitchell. 1996. *Remaking Health Care in America.* San Francisco: Jossey-Bass Publishers.

Sultz, H. and K. Young. 1997. *Health Care USA: Understanding its Organization and Delivery.* Gaithersburg, MD: Aspen Publishers.

MATERIALS MANAGEMENT

Ehrlich, G., and W.H. Springer. 1995. "3rd, Reengineering Material Management Using Computer Technology." *Hospital Material Management Quarterly* 17(1): 65–74.

Giunipero, L.C. 1995. "Reengineering Hospital Material Management." *Hospital Material Management Quarterly* 17(1): 33 40.

Sykucki, T. 1996. "Recent Initiatives in U.S. Hospital Supply Management." *Hospital Material Management Quarterly* 18(3): 32–5.

Weil, T.P. 1996. "Strategies for Material Management Executives." *Hospital Materials Management Quarterly* 18(3) 79–90.

MARKETING

Hallums, A. 1994. "Internal Marketing Within a Health Care Organization: Developing an Implementation Plan." *Journal of Nursing Management* 2(3): 135–42.

MacStravic, S. 1998. "Marketing by Means of the Confidence Factor." *Health Care Strategic Management* 16(1): 1, 19–23.

Naidu, G.M., A. Kleimenhagen, and G.D. Pillari. 1994. "Is Performance Related to Marketing Research in the Health Care Industry?" *Journal of Hospital Marketing* 8(2): 199–225.

Raju, P.S., S.C. Lonial, and Y.P. Gupta. 1995. "Market Orientation and Performance in the Hospital Industry." *Journal of Health Care Marketing* 15(4): 34–41.

Shi, L. 1996. "Analyzing Hospital Market Share Along Product Lines." *Health Services Management Research* 10(3): 137–145.

Wilker, M. 1996. "An Approach to Improving Hospital Advertising." *Journal of Hospital Marketing* 11(1): 53–64.

MEDICAL LIBRARY

Ball, M.J. 1995. "The Library of the Future: An Informatics Institution." *International Journal of Biomedical Computers* 40(2): 85–8.

Brandt, K.A. 1996. "Current Topics in Health Sciences Librarianship." *Bulletin of the Medical Library Association* 84(4): 515–23.

Braude, R.M. 1997. "On the Origin of a Species: Evolution of Health Sciences Librarianship." *Bulletin of the Medical Library Association* 85(1): 1–10.

Frissee, M.E., R.M. Braude, V. Florance, and S. Fuller. 1995. "Informatics and Medical Libraries: Changing Needs and Changing Roles." *Academy of Medicine* 70(1): 30–5.

Jones, C.J. 1993. "Charting a Path for Health Sciences Librarians in an Integrated Information Environment." *Bulletin of the Medical Library Association* 81(4): 421–4.

NURSING/PATIENT CARE SERVICES

Buerhaus, P.I. 1994. "Managed Competition and Critical Issues Facing Nurses." *Journal of Nursing and Health Care* 15(1): 22–6.

Buerhaus, P.I., and D.O. Staiger. 1996. "Managed Care and the Nurse Workforce." *Journal of the American Medical Association* 276(18) 1487–93.

Coile, R.C. 1995. "Nursing Trends 1995–2000." *Russ Coile's Health Trends* 7(7): 1–8.

Donley, R. 1996. "Editorial Comment. Nursing at the Crossroads." *Nursing Economics* 14(6): 325–31.

Hillestad, E.A. 1996. "Nursing in the Year 2000." *Journal of Professional Nursing* (May/June).

Jenkins, R.L. 1997. "Superhighway for the Future of Nursing." *Nurse Educator* 22(3): 44.

Lamm, R.D. 1996. "The Coming Dislocation in the Health Professions." *Healthcare Forum Journal* 39(1): 58–62.

PHARMACY SERVICES

Bonfiglio, M.F. 1997. "A Contemporary Perspective on Pharmacy's Traditional Strengths." *Journal of the American Pharmacy Association* NS37(6): 700–4.

Dukes, G.E. 1997. "Issues and Trends in Clinical Pharmacy Practice, Research, and Education: An Introduction." *Pharmacotherapy* 17(5): 1062.

Felkey, B.G. 1997. "Health System Infomatics." *American Journal of Health Systems Pharmacy* 54(3): 274–80.

Felkey, B.G., and K.N. Barker. 1996. "Technology and Automation in Pharmaceutical Care." *Journal of the American Pharmacy Association* NS36(5): 309–14.

Scott, B. 1997. "Impact of Managed Care in Pharmacy." *Pharmacotherapy* 17(5 Pt. 2): 1555–85.

Zellmer, W.A. 1991. "Editorial. Gaining External Support for Pharmacy's New Mission." *American Journal of Hospital Pharmacy* 48(5): 949.

SOCIAL SERVICES

Dinerman, M. 1997. "Social Work Roles in America's Changing Health Care." *Social Work and Healthcare* 25(1–2): 23–33.

Rosenberg, G. 1994. "Social Work, the Family and the Community." *Social Work and Healthcare* 20(1): 7–20.

Simmons, J. 1994. "Community-Based Care: The New Health Social Work Paradigm." *Social Work and Healthcare* 20(1): 35–46.

Volland, P.J. 1996. "Social Work Practices in Health Care: Looking to the Future with a Different Lens." *Social Work and Healthcare* 24(1–2): 35–51.

INDEX

A

Accountant, 110
Accounting department, 88–90
ACHE, 193–95
ADA, 71
Administrator: duties, 24–25; future role, 26; qualifications, 25–26; staff, 24
Admitting manager, 85
Admitting services, 85–87, 159–60
Affirmative action program, 100–101
Aging population, 188
AHA, 196–97
AIDS, 188
AMA, 198; Code of Medical Ethics, 22; Council on Medical Education, 5, 92; medical education standards, 5
Ambulatory care, 7
American Board of Nuclear Medicine, 50
American College of Healthcare Executives. *See* ACHE
American College of Hospital Administrators, 193
American Dietetic Association. *See* ADA
American Hospital Association. *See* AHA
American Library Association, 69
American Medical Association. *See* AMA
American Medical Record Association. *See* AMRA

American Nurses Association. *See* ANA
American Occupational Therapy Association, 54
American Physical Therapy Association, 55
American Public Health Association. *See* APHA
American Society of Clinical Pathologists. *See* ASCP
American Society of Hospital Pharmacists, 60
American Society of Radiologic Technologists, 45
AMRA, 92
ANA, 32, 199–200
Anatomic pathology, 41
Anesthesia, 4
Annual programs, 104–5
Antiseptic principle, 5
APHA, 201
Architect, 109–10
ASCP, 42
Aseptic surgery, 5
Asset behaviors, 140
Assisted living, 10–11
Associate/assistant director of nursing, 33
Association of Hospital Superintendents, 196
Attorney, 110
Audiovisual service, 73–75
Auditor, 110

About the Authors

Robert M. Sloane, FACHE, is the Director of the Health Administration Program and a Clinical Professor at the University of Southern California. He received a bachelor's degree from Brown University and a master's degree in health administration from Columbia University. In 1996, he was the principal and founder of R. Sloane and Associates, a healthcare consulting firm. He was the president and CEO of V.H.A. West, Inc. in 1995; the president and CEO of Anaheim Memorial Hospital and Foundation from 1986 until 1995; president and CEO of Orthopaedic Hospital and Foundation in Los Angeles from 1980 until 1986; Medical Center administrator and CEO at the City of Hope Medical Center in Duarte, California from 1969 until 1980; associate administrator at Monmouth Medical Center in Long Branch, New Jersey from 1967 until 1969; and assistant director at Yale–New Haven Hospital from 1961 until 1969.

Robert Sloane has served as a board member for a number of hospital associations, including the California Association of Hospitals and Health Systems, the Hospital Council of Southern California (as Chairman in 1985), California Hospitals Political Action Committee (as Chairman in 1983–84), and Voluntary Hospitals of America (as Chairman in 1993 and 1994) He is a Fellow and former Regent of the American College of Healthcare Executives and is a member of the National Advisory Board of the Healthcare Forum. Robert Sloane has been a member of the clinical faculty at the University of Southern California and the University of California at Los Angeles. He has held other teaching faculty positions at Columbia University, Yale University, Quinnipac College, Pasadena City College, California State at Los Angeles, and the California Institute of Technology. In addition to the first three editions of this book, Mr. Sloane has written numerous journal articles.

Beverly LeBov Sloane, FAMWA, is an author, writer, lecturer, and consultant. She received a bachelor's degree from Vassar College and a master's degree from Claremont Graduate University. She is a graduate of the Anderson Graduate School of Management Executive Program at the University of California at Los Angeles and the Stanford University Professional Publishing Course. She was the recipient of a Coro Foundation fellowship for leadership training in public affairs for midcareer women and in 1989 was an Ethics Fellow at Loma Linda University Medical Center.

As a lecturer, Beverly Sloane has presented a workshop on overcoming writer's block for many professional organizations. She has also been an instructor of English literature and creative writing at Monmouth College in West Long Branch, New Jersey. In addition to being a coauthor of the first three editions of this book, she is the coauthor of a humorous cookbook, *From Vassar to Kitchen.* Beverly Sloane is also a Fellow of the American Medical Writers Association. She was a delegate to the national board of the organization for many years and has also served as President of the Pacific Southwest Chapter, National Chairman of the Freelance Section, and National Administrator of Sections. In addition, she has served both as State President and as President of the Los Angeles Chapter of California Press Women. She was named California Communicator of Achievement in 1992. She was a member of the national board of the National Federation of Press Women and served as National Director of the Speakers Bureau for that organization. In 1992, she was named first runner-up as National Communicator of Achievement. Beverly Sloane also served as Vice President of Community Affairs for Women in Communication, Inc. In 1986, she was named Woman of Achievement–Woman of the Year by the Arcadia, California, branch of the American Association of University Women.

Richard K. Harder is the senior training consultant with the Employers Group, a not-for-profit human resource consulting and training association based in California. His work involves developing and presenting in-company and public leadership, management and supervisory educational programs in both healthcare and non–healthcare organizations. Mr. Harder also consults with management on organizational issues and problems that can be resolved through management education and organizational development strategies.

Mr. Harder has held administrative, management, human resource development, and consulting positions in healthcare organizations over the past 25 years. Prior positions Mr. Harder has held include training and development manager, management development trainer, regional director of professional development and vice president of human resources. He has held leadership positions at the following Southern California healthcare institutions: City of Hope National Medical Center, Duarte; Huntington Memorial Hospital, Pasadena; Queen of the Valley Hospital, West Covina; and Inter-Community Medical Center, Covina.

Mr. Harder is an adjunct professor in the school of organizational management at the University of La Verne, La Verne, California, where he teaches at the graduate and undergraduate levels in the school of health services administration.

He earned a master's degree in healthcare management at California State University, Los Angeles. He earned undergraduate degrees in business administration from California State University, San Francisco, and in hotel and restaurant management from the City College of San Francisco.